Published by:

THE PROFESSIONAL IMAGE, inc.
    In the U.S: South Beach and South Florida
    International: St. Croix, St. Thomas, Tortola, St. Maarten, Aruba
    CONTACT US AT: the_professional_image@yahoo.com

"UNDERNEATH A CLOUDLESS SKY"

ISBN: 978-0-615-32877-5

THANKS TO OUR STAFF:

EDITOR: EILEEN CLARK

PHOTOGRAPHS: THE PROFESSIONAL IMAGE, INC.,
    David McMahan and J. Christopher Photography...
    You can see more of their work at;
    http://www.davidmcmahan.com/
    or www.jchristopherphotography.com

Copyright © 2010 by Michael Bennett~the Tropical Cuisinier!
All rights reserved. No part of this publication may be reproduced, distributed, or transmitted in any form or by any means, including photocopying, recording, or other electronic or mechanical methods, without the prior written permission of the publisher, except in the case of brief quotations embodied in critical reviews and certain other noncommercial uses permitted by copyright law. For permission requests, write to the publisher, addressed "Attention: Permissions Coordinator," at the address below.
The Professional Image, inc.
3950 N 56th Ave., Suite 309
Hollywood, Fl. 33021

ORDERING INFORMATION:
Quantity sales. Special discounts are available on quantity purchases by corporations, associations, and others. For details, contact the publisher at the address above.
Orders by U.S. trade bookstores and wholesalers. Please contact TPI Distribution: Tel: 305-851-3441

Printed in the United States of America

My heart belongs to my family because they have followed me as I follow my *PASSION* to the Caribbean.

FoodBrats.Com

To get this book on Cd-Rom, as an E-book, or as a FLASH reader file at an incredible

Price

go to our website:

www.foodbrats.com

Chef Michael Bennett, is the Tropical Cuisinier!

Chef Michael's culinary status has been highlighted in publications that include The New York Times, Ocean Drive Magazine, National Culinary Review, Zagat Review ("best of"), as well as many other newspaper and magazine features. He has appeared on several television cooking shows including The Today Show-South Florida.

Miami New Times magazine featured Michael as one of South Florida's pivotal figures in the use of exotic tropical food.

11-09

UNDERNEATH A CLOUDLESS SKY

....IS A COMPILATION OF RECIPES COLLECTED FROM MY CULINARY JOURNEYS THROUGH SOUTH FLORIDA AND THE CARIBBEAN.

I have brought these recipes to you through years of evaluation and planning. Being from South Florida, I was immersed into the Caribbean cookery heritage through my entire culinary career. I admired these new cookery traditions so much that I relocated with my family 1600 miles away to the tropics.

After spending four years in the Caribbean, I have returned with a greater understanding of how everyday cooking has evolved into what is known today as Caribbean Fusion or, "Caribb-ican" ~ as a chef once described it to me in the Caribbean.

BOOK OVERVIEW

Chefs on the New American Riviera have created a culinary fusion cuisine that is based on all of our five distinct culinary heritages. This multi-cultural cuisine category is a Five Flags conglomerative cuisine. Each of these Five Flags represents a societal group of South Florida residents. This impact coerces a South Florida chef's culinary interpretation resulting in this wondrous bounty of dining choices. By fusing our locally-grown tropical, exotic food pantry with the melding of multiple Caribbean and American - North, South and Latin American - culinary heritages, it is no wonder that this Cuisine was called the most adventurous in the country.

The most noticeable trait of our new American regional cuisine is its complexities of tastes, with extremes in exotic boldness. Distinct, and various individual cultural cookery heritages from Caribbean Basin nations are united within each new recipe. The chef will daily infuses his/her menu with a multitude of flavor varieties with multi-cultural cookery techniques and then elevates the dining experience to a level of "metropolitan" sophistication. South Florida chefs will tell their patrons that their food is going to explode with colors on the plate, as well as, bold tastes on the palate.

The use of an eccentric tropical pantry of spices and exotic sounding foodstuffs to produce bold flavors has been intertwined into this multi-cultural cookery cuisine. Just as a fine wine develops different characteristics from differing soil conditions and a changes of micro climates, so do many of the exotic tropical products harvested in south Florida. The mango can be a topic of much discussion here because being that there are 2500 different varieties of mango worldwide, each of these mangos produces differing tastes in a finished plate.

Of course, with 800 miles of Florida coastline, South Florida menus are regularly interspersed with a wide spectrum of seafood choices. Chefs treat our seafood bounty as if it never left the Ocean, pairing these super-fresh ingredients with the exotic tastes from our Caribbean-inspired tropical pantry.

Hopefully, my passion will soon be one that stimulates you to explore more and more throughout the next few hours, days and weeks....

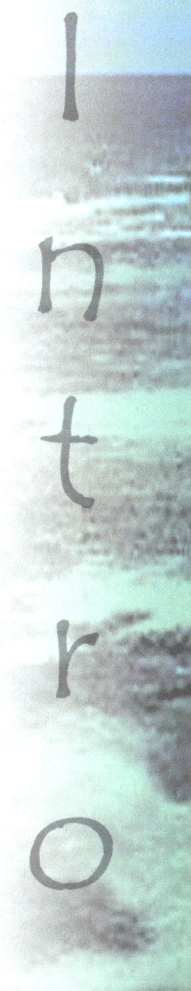

A Chef's Passion is...
by The Tropical Cuisinier!

...what is or has been important in one's own life.

...it drives us for more.

...it encourages the betterment of ourselves.

...it overrides other motives for its own fulfillment.

...it discourages stagnation.

...it drives us to pursue the seemingly once unattainable.

...it unrealistically fulfills one's life with obtainable platitudes.

...it overrides or blurs out important real life issues, concerns and needs.

Aspirations for greatness develop from...

Passion!

AND THE JOURNEY BEGINS....

As you are opening this book, we start our journey into the vast tropical regions of the world. Our journey will start at the southernmost tip of Florida, cruise down to the Leeward Islands, go west to South America and travel back home across the Gulf of Mexico generating this large triangle we call the Caribbean Basin.

Our journey together is also based on the premise that you are looking for something different to cook for dinner tonight. This journey begins as you flip through the pages of this book and will end with your family's amazement at tonight's dinner.

You are now embarking upon a journey of freedom.

I will begin our trek by setting the scene for you. Imagine a beautiful "Cloudless Sky". The panorama before you is a tropical azure sky touching an even more beautiful blue-green sea. Warm breezes are always wafting towards you from the east. They bring with them a steamy essence of the tropics. You are now just beginning to appreciate my journey into the Caribbean.

The passages within this book will tell you a story of what it is like to be in this exotic region. It is a mind-set dominated by use of exotic food and boundless culinary freedoms. The freedom to invent combinations of tastes and cross-cultural culinary wizardry that are not constrained by an American "regional" cookery stereotypes. You are now in the nation of innovation.

Tropical journey realized....

Any expedition usually starts at an airport. Ours doesn't. We are going to travel sans jet propulsion. I have journeyed to many of these island nations living and working as a chef. This book will enable you to investigate what it is like to be a chef within these eternal territories within your own kitchen.

Here in South Florida, chefs aren't bound by previous regional cookery preferences. We assess the dining preferences of our multi-cultural community and then stylize menus for this base of residents. Since this area is alive with the immigrants of the Caribbean, it only makes sense for restaurateurs to offer a myriad of Caribbean influenced foods. This is how I have prepared my recipes for the past thirty years.

This culinary passion has taken me to the tropical regions of the world. You will understand this passion in my writing and then the presentations between the circumferences of the plate.

This is how I have cultivated the menu styling of this book. This edification and pseudo-travel is now yours without having to buy a ticket on a jetliner. It is a culinary journey without restraints~without physical boundaries...

"FAMILIARITY BREEDS CONTEMPT."

Not so! Familiarity brings comfort and reassurance, while trying new things. I will bring unfamiliar exotic food and cooking techniques into focus for you. After reading this book you will be more comfortable using food your mother would have never considered cooking.

As creatures of habit, most people resist change. We are uncomfortable with the unknown. After a decade of experimentation, I have developed ways to minimized your risk of cooking something un-common. I have developed a method of pairing the unknown with something most of you will be comfortable cooking. In this book, I am going to guide you through this probe with adventurous fervor.

As creatures of habit, we get comfortable cooking the same things over and over again. With so much practice, it becomes easier to cook with little wasted time or steps. The only problem with this theory is that the average home cook has a repertoire of only ten dishes. There are only seven days in the week that should be plenty, right? Well for most Americans, repetitious of home cooked meals is the number one reason why families go out to eat.

I will guide you through a naturally arrived system of exploring new taste tempting ideas. When I first started experimenting with exotic tropical foods, I was also a novice. It took many years of failing before I found how to successfully mix and mingle certain foods on the plate to develop a balanced "Taste-Variance".

Every person looking for a new cookbook is looking for new sense impression for their tastebuds. I will provide you an opportunity to learn and create new taste variances that many people in America will never have the good fortune to experience. You will now be able to bedazzle your guests with exotic tropical flavors and pairings that they will talk to their friends about for years to come.

I hope you will enjoy reading this book as much as I have had writing it.

The Tropical Cuisinier!

Contents

Intro .... page 4

Chapter One—Insight and Background
FYI Glossary
What is it that makes the Teflon City what it is today.............................page 12
The Kampong ....pages 13-14
Cooking essentials...page 15
New Cooking ingredients...pages 16-18
A Spa perception ....page 19
Tropical cookery provisions...page 20
Florida facts ....page 21
Early Florida Agriculture..page 22-23
Culinary uses ....pages 23-37

Chapter Two—Starters and Bouchees
Recipes ....pages 37-53

Chapter Three—Salads
The Redlands..pages 55-56
The Morning Market..pages 56-57
Recipes..pages 58-64

Chapter Three and a half—the "Zip"
Dressings and Such..page 65
Salad Essentials..pages 66-69
Recipes..pages 70-75

Chapter Four—le Repertoire
Duplicating foodways..page 77-78
Deco...pages 78-80
Recipes..pages 81-89

Chapter Five—Sauces
Tastes, a scientific look...pages 91-93
Recipes..pages 95-112

Chapter Six–Scales and Fins

- Buying fish..pages 115-116
- South Florida Aquaculture..page 117
- Shellfish...pages 118-120
- Stoners..page 121
- Fish Characteristics...page 122
- Recipes..pages 123-141

Chapter Seven–Feathers and Bones

- Recipes..pages 143-156

Chapter Eight–Starchy Things

- Starches, defined..pages 160-163
- Recipes..pages 164-182

Index...pages 183-185

Insight and Background

...cooking on the
"New American Riviera".

WHAT IS IT THAT MAKES THE "MAGIC CITY" WHAT IT IS TODAY?

Being fashionably different! This is easily seen in the influx of new and differing restaurant menu concepts.

One ingredient on these menus that is fast becoming more recognizable is the mango. This fruit is even utilized by some of the most retro, 1950's living, Ward Cleavers. The mango is fast becoming as common as the apple in the daily pantry of Cleaver-esque South Floridians.

With the same excitement that a mango imparts, a festival is held every year to celebrate this unique food. The International Mango Festival held in Coral Gables (a Miami suburb) is the largest event of its kind in this hemisphere. This international event happens every year on the second weekend in July.

Dr. Richard Campbell, the organizer of this event, along with a contingent of local notable chefs, helped bring into prominence something called a "Horizontal Mango Tasting". It is similar to a horizontal wine tasting in nature where a panel of four chefs discuss the differing taste traits of five varieties of mango. Later, the "Vertical Tasting" summarizes the different tastes of a mango through the phases of its ripeness.

"I have been doing this event for five years now with Dr. Campbell. Our audiences really love it", says a chef on the panel. One year, the nationally recognized Robin Haas stole the show with his interpretation of how to eat a mango...naked in the bathtub. (Robin always has something amusing to add to the panel's evaluations.)

The audience loves the commentary provided about each mango variety. They take notes as the chefs describe a mango's tastes, textures, and other attributes. A chef related to me once that: "One year my wife was looking over onto her neighbor's wristwatch to see what time it was, and her neighbor protectively covered her notes. She thought my wife was trying to steal her scribbled secrets." These are real mango-holics at these events. The King of Fruit deserves loyalty, but these people are about to give up a virginal sacrifice for our new cooking tips.

THE KAMPONG

The sound of the wind rushing through a vast melange of tropical fruit trees screens a spirited rendition of Mozart.

The sun is warm, on this beginning day of May. Blankets are lazily spread over grassy knolls that overlook the Bay of Biscayne. Participants begin to relish today's South Florida delicacies, as a slight breeze blows off the water bring with it the scent of the nearby Atlantic ocean. Watching a few archaic wooden sailing Yachts drift by, one is brought back to their senses by a passing jet. The cultured, yet relaxed atmosphere makes for a pleasant day. Few places combine these cosmopolitan characteristics with such natural beauty. As the day progresses, gulls and pelicans soar over the waters of Biscayne bay searching for today's snack, while you have been enjoying the food of Miami's top chefs.

The "Kampong", translates into "a small cluster of homes". It is the location for today's event. This location, is just a short drive from America's own exotic "Napa Valley" - the Redlands. This was the home of Dr. David Fairchild, the man responsible for the uniqueness of today's South Florida Cuisine. He had started South Florida's first tropical fruit plantation not far from here. Starting in 1926, he brought back a multitude of unknown tropical plants (from his explorations of Equatorial countries) and transplanted them here. A relatively short list of the foods he brought back included: mango, papaya, atemoya, jackfruit, pomelo, passionfruit, and mamey. Because South Florida is sub-tropical, tropical fruit from around the globe can, and do, grow here well. South Florida is the only place in the adjacent United States that has this capability.

South Florida chefs have a passion for newness and make use of these nouveau tropical food specialties - in not yearly, or seasonally - but daily changing menus. It is a cuisine that has been formatted personally by the chef, focusing on freshness and depth of a unique tropical flavor. South Florida chefs are challenged everyday to create stunning dishes that use this array of diverse exotic tropical ingredients that originally were brought to this area by Dr. Fairchild.

South Florida chefs extract the maximum out of these tropical delicacies by using a "Spa-style" cooking technique. Cream laden preparations don't over-whelm the exotic nature of these tropically-inspired dishes by masking them with excessive fatty sauces. The use of light purees, coulis, and "Coulis-grettes" to enliven a dish's taste are a main stay with South Florida chefs. Our most noteworthy chefs are still exploiting the creative freedom they inherited from the 1980's and the new American regional cookery movement.

My interpretation of this – I have deemed "Florida's Five Flags Fusion Foods". F.F.F.F.F. uses these rare fruits and vegetables as the basis of any my new menus. Our exotic and tropical menu "trademark" is now our "monopoly". Unknowingly, Dr. Fairchild created the fuel for a machine that has produced the Florida's Five Flags Fusion Foods.

Off in the distance, one can see the trappings of millionaire mansions, but the Kampong has a wealth all its own. The teak bench that overlooks this Bay is a marvelous place to feel the warmth of the South Florida sunshine and an occasional spray from tropical waters. Many come to this place-where the lush tropical vegetation touches the waters of Biscayne Bay-to relax and collect their thoughts, but few realize the reason for the commencement of this affair. It is to celebrate a way of life, bringing together a perfect spring day with the "hottest" new Tropical cuisine styling in America.

COOKING ESSENTIALS...

These are a few examples on what your kitchen should be kept in stock.

A nonstick pan: this can be as good as you like, but a simple Teflon 9-10 inch saute pan will do in many circumstances.

Coffee-grinder: for grinding freshly roasted spices and fresh ground pepper.

Hand blender: this is like having an "Osterizer" on a stick. It is a lot more portable and you don't have to transfer liquids in a out of the blender.

A heavy bottom stainless steel pot: it might seem unnecessary, but they are worth every penny when it comes to making sauces properly.

Food processor. Enough said.

Wok (with a smoker rack attachment): once you have used one, there won't be any turning back. It is versatile enough for any circumstance; plus, with a smoker attachment, it can be used in place of a wood-fire grill to add extra-flavors.

Chinoise: fine mesh strainer, it is essential in a modern kitchen.

Wooden spoon: for stirring without damaging the bottom of Teflon pan.

Plastic-"Rubbermaid"-spatula: great for getting every last drop of a sauce or dressing.

Pastry spatula: great for delicate small servings.

Zester: if you are going to add flavors of citrus fruits to anything, the best way is to use their zest.

Whips: fine "piano" wire whips, great for stirring and blending sauces and dressings completely.

And, of course, where would you be without a good sharp set of knives?

NEW COOKING INGREDIENTS/TERMS:

Acidic Water - water with a little lemon juice added to prevent browning of fruit.

Annatto/Achiote - a berry from a plant that grows well here. It is simmered in oil and strained out to produce a coloring agent. Used in Arroz con Pollo.

Atemoya - Possibly the greatest tasting fruit on earth. Tastes of vanilla, pineapple and custard. Available August thorough October. 3/4 lb. average weight per fruit. .

Awark and Caribe Indians - the first natives on the Caribbean Islands.

Barbados cherry-soft, juicy, thin red skinned fruit with a orange flesh that is high in Vitamin C. Available April thorough November.

Batido - a (tropical) fruit puree milk shake.

Breadfruit - Versatile, use with beer batter for frying. When over ripe use in soups and sweet coconut dishes. High in carbohydrates. Tastes vaguely of applesauce when cooked. Use as a veggy-cook as a potato when hard green. This is why Captain Bligh made his journey to Polynesia.

Black Sapote, or chocolate pudding fruit - it has a soft, rich, fudge-like flesh with a green outer skin turning olive in color as it ripens. Available December to January.

Blueberries - available in Central Florida May first.

Boniato - Cook as a potato. Has a hard dry texture and taste of chestnuts. Available most of the year.

Brine - solution used to preserve foods. Pepper brine is usually a vinegar.

Calamondin - Orange fleshed, acidic pulp, smaller than an orange in size. Extremely sweet-tart. Available December through September.

Calabaza - Aztec and Mayan specialty squash. Green to orange skin, flesh is orange in color. Available May through January. Flesh and seeds are edible, good source of Vitamin A.

Canistel - When cooked, texture is like an egg yolk, hence the name "Egg custard fruit". Comes from Central America. Available throughout the winter months. High in carbohydrates. Use when ripe, and overly soft in custards and ice creams or as a veggie when hard.

"Coulis-grette" - a fruit puree (Coulis) that has been enhanced with a light flavored vinegar. Then an appropriate oil is added to smooth its palatability (vinaigrette).

Cherimoya - Custardy sweet juicy pulp, taste of slightly papaya, pineapple and banana. Available December to May. No sodium. Average weight 1/2 pound.

Chimichurri - see recipe.

Cholesterol free - less than 2 milligrams of cholesterol per serving.

Colada - coffee served at little Cuban snack shops throughout South Florida. Most of us cannot get through a day without it.

Dasheen - from China. Creamy color flesh with lavender specs in the pulp. Taste of artichokes and chestnuts. Cook like a potato.

Florida Polenta - Grits with cheese.

Grilling techniques -

    Start with paper or kindling.

    Heat wood or coals to gray before cooking foods.

    Always oil slats.

    Use water soaked fresh herbs for flavored smoke. Also use for brushing with a marinade or basting sauces.

Grits and Grunts - a mandatory breakfast for most true coastal Southerners.

Guavas - Use raw, or made into stews, jam, jellies and a paste.

Guarapo - Sugar cane juice. Squeezed fresh out of the stalks of sugarcane with a special machine that crushes the stalks to release their juices. Found in most Latin snack shops. Use as an marinade for seafood. Reduce over heat to a get syrup for sauces.

Infusion - adding a concentrated flavor to a broth, oil or vinegar.

Jaboticaba - dark green, grape-like fruit ripening to purple originating from Brazil. Grows from the trunk of the tree not at the end of the branch. Available March thru June.

Kumquats - Intense orange flavor. Skin and flesh edible and should be eaten together at one time. Another import from China. High in Vitamin C and A.

Lemongrass -freezes well, used to flavor broths, marinades, sauces, vinegars and curries. Called fever grass in the Caribbean.

Longan (Tiger-eyes) - Oriental import, native of S.E. Asia. Came to Florida in the '40's. Available June thorough July. Good with Seafood. High in Vitamin C. Only 66 calories per 10 fruit.

Loquat, the Japanese plum - Oval, Apricot-looking in appearance fruit. Surprisingly good taste from this orange-colored flesh fruit. Available July to August.

Lichee (Litchi) - 2nd century B.C. Chinese emperors's favorite. Available only from the second week of June to the second week of July (with some varieties from Mexico available onto the third week of July). Freeze and eat like a Sorbet without processing. High in Vitamin C. Low in Sodium.

Macadamia nuts - grows sparsely in South Florida. Buttery flavor, soft, fruity. Has hard or papery shells.

Malanga - Pink, yellow or cream colored. Tastes like musty potatoes. Cook as you would potatoes. Choose the ones with hard outside textures and no soft spots.

Mamey - Available in the fall in South Florida. Use soft-ripe. Taste of maple-sweet potato-melon. Use with rum sauce, ice cream and other frozen yogurt desserts.

Mojo - Seville orange juice, garlic, herbs and oil.

Old Sour - Lime juice used as a seasoning.

Purple asparagus - available from California second week of April.

Reduction (natural) - Reducing quantities of fluids by evaporation over heat. Always develop flavors by intense reductions.

Sapodilla (Naseberries) - Flesh is honey blonde in color, grainy texture like a pear. Seeds not edible. Sweet maple flavored pulp. Use them ripe in desserts, salads and frozen Ices. Available March-July.

Seville Orange - looks like a sweet orange with a rougher exterior. It has at times a extremely sour-bitter taste. Used in making cream de Curraco (named for the Caribbean Island nation where it was made famous). Also the main ingredient used in Orange marmalade.

Shellac - a glazing sauce used to give a shine. Use just as would wood shellac.

Shiitake Mushrooms-grown in Ocala.

Soursop - flavored like a custard-pineapple-mango with a tart richness. It's outer flesh looks prehistoric with soft, spikelike protrusions covering the entire fruit.

Spa cuisine - lighter style of cooking using low-fat, salt and cholesterol.

"Ugli-fruit" - a cross between a grapefruit and a tangerine. Its name is because of its loose fitting skin.

A SPA PERCEPTION

WHAT IS SPA CUISINE?

To many people, it is the elimination of fats and the other unhealthy elements of cooking. To most, the elimination of cholesterol and saturated fats are of utmost importance. It is all of this and more.

First, let us mention what these "Spa" guidelines means...

Fats and their elimination concern the removal of ADDITIONAL fats to lean (fat) foods. While writing this book, I limit the use of additional saturated fats.

As a guide, most saturated fats are solid at room temperature. Any fats from an animal source, whether it be cream, butter, cheese, caul fat, suet, clarified chicken fat, etc... are all saturated and cholesterol. To this list we have to add the saturated plant (tropical) oils: coconut, palm, rapeseed, etc....

Saturated fats help raise the cholesterol levels in your blood. Since your body has all the cholesterol it will ever need, the excess that you eat is stored by your body along the inner walls of your arteries. This excess buildup around the blood vessels and restricts blood flow. The lack of blood to certain parts of body tissue causes it to be less nourished and eventually the tissues die. If this tissue is on the heart, that part of the heart stops working and causes a heart attack.

Secondly, spa cuisine guides us to a more health conscious way of nourishing oneself. These are the guidelines that Spa cuisine sets to improve our cooking practices...

Use only vegetable oils; mono-unsaturated (Olive oil) or, polyunsaturated (Safflower oil).

Substitute concentrated fruit juices in place of oils for salad dressing, marinades, and sauces.

Substitute naturally reduced sauces for Roux (butter) thickened ones.

Make use of flavorings such as herb combinations, spices blends, or chilies to replace salt as a flavor enhancer.

Use rice, grains, and other starches to replace the protein (usually rich in fat) in the plate composition.

Use low-in-fat seafood and game entrees.

Use fat substitution ingredients that have been modified by the producer, such as non-fat sour cream and yogurt.

Use chutneys, various pickles, relishes, salsa's and other condiments

Tropical Provisions

Some of these products are

grown in South Florida and some originate from other places in the Caribbean.

Florida facts

Just a few quick facts about Florida...a land of plenty.

Florida is the number one agricultural state in the Southeast.
Florida ranks number two in veggie production in the United States.
Florida's beef industry is also number two in the United States in calf production.
Florida's top dollar farmed products are;

Oranges-	$1.15 billion.
Tomatoes-	$571 million.
Sugarcane-	$483 million.
Grapefruit-	$309 million.
Potatoes-	$163 million.
Sweet corn-	$91 million.
Watermelons-	$80 million.
Limes-	$26 million.
Avocados-	$13 million.

Florida also has many other interesting production statistics. Florida produces the highest percentages of products grown in the nation. A few of these fruits and veggies are;

Tangelos-	100%
Temples-	100%
Limes-	95.3%
Grapefruit-	81.1%
Oranges-	68.9%
Tomatoes-	62.1%
Sugarcane-	56.4%

After looking over these statistics we can see that when Florida has a hurricane, or even worse, a state-wide freeze, the entire nation suffers. If Florida looses production in any of these items, most of our national production is lost.

EARLY FLORIDA AGRICULTURE

As agricultural development experts (for third world countries) travel around the world, they talk to developing agricultural countries using our South Floridian agricultural situation as a worst case scenario. Because South Florida sits atop a limestone aquifer, in many locations throughout South Florida, we have only 18 inches of top soil. After you dig away the top soil, you have to blast a hole in the limestone to plant a sizable tree. Many deep-rooted trees such as the mango, sapote, lichee and avocado can not get the proper depth in which they need to grow. This leads to our secondary condition that puts South Florida's fruit trees in peril.

Since the trees do not have a deep root system, they do not have a stable base in which to anchor themselves. As we experienced in 1992, when hurricane Andrew passed thorough, the trees with little to hold onto were uprooted. When the roots are exposed to the winds and the blowing saltwater of a passing hurricane, they die.

Spanish lime, sugar apple, and guava originally grew wild on the outskirts of Miami. In 1890, the tropical plant industry was started in South Florida with a 7 acre experimental garden. The original area was part of an old airfield. The "Haden" mango was the first tropical plant started there. The Haden, being one of the best tasting of all mangos, is a cross between the Indian "Mulgoba" and the "Turpentine". Both were chosen for this area because of their ability to flourish in hostile growing conditions. Other popular varieties of South Florida mangos are the "Keitt", the "Kent" and the "Glenn". Later in the next century the "Tommy Akins" was developed in the backyard of a Fort Lauderdale resident, Tommy Akins. The Akins are now being planted throughout the world now because of its ability to withstand variances in latitudinal movement.

Florida has long been known as one of the world's greatest producers of oranges, but among the world's most popular fruits, the mango is Florida's most prized. The total South Florida acreage devoted to growing tropical fruits, only the avocado comes close to mango with lichees and longans not far behind.

Many professional people have retired to South Florida and helped develop this acreage. The backyard and non-professional growers who are interested in preserving and increasing the numbers of tropical fruits grown in South Florida are the people experimenting with these exotic foods.

Culinary Uses

F
Y
I

Culinary uses

ANNONA

This section deals with a family of fruit because of their general similarities. The family of Annona is similarly grouped by looks, taste, texture and size. Most Annona are related by their similarity in custard-y flesh. All have similar seed dispersal. Most have the pineapple-custardy-vanilla taste. When you see any member of this family hanging from a tree, you will definitely stop and look. Family members are: atemoya, rollinia, cherimoya, pond apple. sugar apple (sweet sop), sour sop, illama and bullock's heart.

The Annona is the first recorded New World fruit. This product isn't indigenous to South Florida, but it grows here easily. I believe that this family of fruit is the most sensual in the tropical fruit realm. The uses for this group are also similar. The flesh is slightly granular. They can be eaten out of hand, used in a salad, soup, sauce, coulis-grettes, compotes, as a dessert topping, in an anglaise, into waffles, with seafood and as an ice cream. Every member of this family can be used throughout the tropical world. They have been the fruit of choice of South Americans since before the time of Christ. Even Mark Twain wrote of Cherimoya as...." Heaven's perfect gift". The most important thing about these fruits is they can't tolerate cold temperatures - a true example of a "tropical" fruit. South Florida is in the extreme northern boundary of their growing region. Varieties like the cherimoya - like higher elevations and in Florida where they grow smaller.

To Use:

    Make sure they feel like an overripe banana. The skin splits easily and they have many seeds that have to be dispensed. As you cut them, place in an acidic solution (water with a squeeze of lime juice) to help them from discoloring. As you peel back the skin with a knife their fragrance wafts upward. This is something that everyone should experience at least a dozen times a week.

Not so long ago, the "kiwi" was an unknown food product. With its successful marketing, it was used by nearly every chef in this country in the '70s and early '80s. New fruits such as these will have to be marketed in much the same manner to make them as popular as mangos are now. It may take some time, but after they are experienced, there will be no question that this group of fruit will become more popular as they are used by cooks who like to experiment.

Distinctions:

Atemoya - cross of cherimoya and sugar apple. Convex bumps.

Cherimoya - concave, scalelike round exterior. Wild varieties are more conical-heart shaped.

Illama - more round in shape with a stronger custard flavor.

Rollinia - two times the size of atemoya. Similar shape, look and taste.

Sour sop - more tart, pineapple flavor, heart shaped with protruding nodes.

Sugar apple (Sweet Sop) - smaller, bumpy scales, round outside. Very sweet more so than the rest. The "scales" (fruit divisions) separate when ripe.

Each variety available at different times of the year, though.

Most all family members are harvested in the fall and winter months. Most are high in both calcium and phosphorus

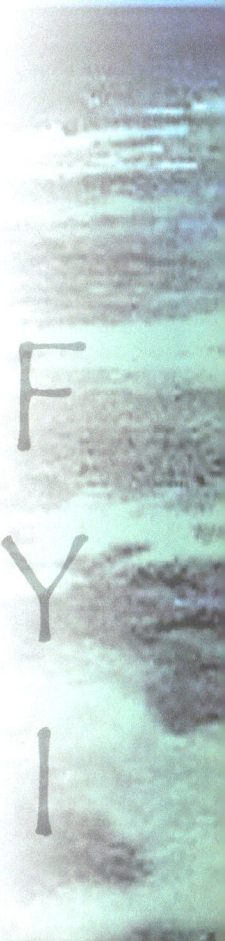

Culinary Uses

BONIATO, the real Sweet potato

You might think you know what a sweet potato is but, hold on. One of the new World's most important contributions to the old World is the potato. The boniato is the South American sweet potato. The yam that we have every Thanksgiving is exactly that-a yam.

The sweet potato originated in the Andes Mountains, where the natives have been cultivating them for more than two thousand years. The world's first cultivated tuber is the fourth most popular cash crop in the world. The earliest Spanish explorers named this product BONIATO because it was safe to eat.

These tubers are available year round in South Florida. Don't refrigerate, and store no longer than a few days. Look for skins that range in colors of pink, purple, cream and red and make sure they don't have any soft spots.

To Use:
> Use as you would any Idaho potato. They make excellent fried chips (served with salsa). They can also be baked, added to soups, stews or in puddings. Remember to keep in water as you cut the surfaces. It will brown if you don't.

The Boniato has 115 calories per 1/2 cup with a good amount of vitamin A.

Culinary Uses

CARAMBOLA, the Starfruit

Starfruit, as it is more popularly known, has actually been grown here since the early 1920's. Transplanted from the jungles of Indo-China, at least five different commercial varieties now grow here. An important crop for Oriental medicines, it has been used as a digestive agent for hundreds of years.

It is available twice a year, from late August to February and May through June, in South Florida. There are lesser used varieties that grow at different times of the year. These species are being used to stretch the growing and production season .

To Use:
Just slice and eat. Or, peel off the slightly brown tips of the ribs and peel the light, almost plasticine outer flesh and slice or eat out of hand. Seeds are minimal, if any. Use in place of any lemon or lime called for in a recipe, though the Starfruit is more delicate in flavor. Wrap lightly in wax paper and its shelf life in the refrigerator (at around 40 degrees) is a week.

In southern Chinese cuisines, starfruit are used as a digestive and are eaten before meats or, as the "sour" in place of tamarind or lime - in sweet and sour sauces. They can also be used in many other ways: as a substitute for any sour taste in a recipe in sorbet, bavarians, ices, compotes, marmalades, as plate garnishes; for chutneys; salsa dressings; coulis-grettes; for liquors, flavored wines and vinegars; and salads. Books have been written on the various culinary uses for this product alone.

3.5 oz. of starfruit has only has only 33 calories and is high in vitamin C and has 155.0 ug units of beta-carotene.

<u>Varieties available....</u>
Sweet....Arkin, Fwang Tung, Thai Knight, Maha, Yougans
Tart....Golden Star, Thayer, Newcombe, Star King

Culinary uses

GUAVA

Guavas have grown wild in South Florida for more than a century. Many people in the undeveloped areas of South Florida have guava trees growing in their "back-forty". Florida is our nation's largest producer of guava.

A fragrant fruit originating in the American tropics, there are more than 150 differing varieties worldwide. The variety that is most prevalent here is the small green or yellow sphere. The inside flesh is pink and it has many seeds. Choose the slightly soft ones or let ripen for a few days on the kitchen window sill. The scent of the ripening guava will perfume your kitchen.

Fruits ripen on trees in stages....so it might takes months to harvest all the ripe fruit.

To Use:
Scoop out the inner flesh and heat to facilitate the removal of these seeds. Strain the pulp and use in sauces, marinades, vinegars, mousses, sorbets, dressings, coulis and chutneys. The rind can be used blanched and saved for up to one year in the freezer.

A guava fruit has about 45 calories and is high in vitamin C.
Available mostly September through January

Culinary uses

LITCHI (Lichee)

Litchi is probably South Florida's most sought-after summer fruit. It only has a one-month window to be harvested. In the year 200 B.C., a Chinese Emperor made the Litchi a sought after commodity by having them pony expressed them to the royal palace as they turned ripe. Obviously this was before the time of the freezer, because if he ever tried one frozen, he might have changed his mind. One of my favorite ways to eat the litchi is straight out of it's shell right from the freezer. South Floridians freeze this tropical delight and consume it like shelled sorbet.

Of course the optimal way of eating one is fresh off the tree, but with its hard shell, they keep extremely well for short periods of time. South Florida has a few varieties of Litchi. The first and most common is the single-seeded litchi. I consider this one better because of the fact that the Brewser variety has a more musty flavor. The Brewser, with a few (orange seed-sized) seeds, is prized more by Asians. The flesh is white and like a grape in texture with a sugary flavor.

This product can grow in South Florida because of our sub-tropical climate, and is also a major U.S. supplier of litchis from the United States. Being a favorite among Oriental peoples, litchi has become a major cash crop in the Redlands. You won't have to go to the extremes that the Chinese emperors did to enjoy litchis, but I think when you taste one, you will agree that 1.4 billion Chinese can't be wrong.

To Use:
They can be used in more ways than I can write about here, but a few of them include: poultry and pork dishes, ice creams, sorbet, bavarians, shakes, creme caramels, salads and salad dressings, flavored vinegars, liquors and with grain dishes.

1 cup of Litchi has about 125 calories and provide 225% of the Vitamin C you need on a daily basis.

Available mid-June to mid-July.

Culinary Uses

MALANGA

Malanga is not much to look at, but its versatility is a major reason for its popularity. More than 1.7 million boxes are sold in South Florida per year. This vegetable has been used for more than 2000 years, and was first used as a starch by the Chinese before rice.

This product has many names and uses. In the Bahamas, it is called cxocoyam, the Latins of Central America call it yautia and it is called malanga (or tannia) in South Florida. Pick the ones without blemishes and soft spots. Wear gloves while trimming its shaggy brown skin, then place them in water and let soak. Keep them submerged until you are ready to use. Most malanga weigh about a half pound. It is an inexpensive source of starch and has a nutty flavor that is not found in most members of the tuber family.

To Use:
Like most tubers it has many uses that include: fritters, mashed, boiled, in soups, salads, casseroles and as a foil for rich foods. Frying it as a chip is commonly used here. It can also be used as a coating like other tubers in a preparation for fried oysters. Enhancement by other products balances out the neutral taste of this product.

Available most of the year. Each 1/2 cup of cooked malanga has about 135 calories and is high in thiamine, riboflavin, vitamin C and iron.

Culinary Uses

MANGO

This page will probably be the least necessary of all in this section due to the popularity of the mangos throughout the world. Mangos have crossed the marketing and popularity boundaries that restrict most other tropical "exotics" in this chapter. We have more than seven different commercially-harvested varieties, although there are more than 250 different South Florida varieties.

Mangos originated in the area between India and Vietnam, where the best variety, the Cambodian mango is found. There are 1500 different varieties of mango with new crossbreds are just a cross-pollination away. Every time cross pollinations occur between different mango varieties, a new type of mango is born. Known as the "King of Fruit", mangos have a loyal following with many different cultures. Mangos are the "passion of Summer" harvested in the summertime in the months of June through October.

To Use:
Mangos can be used in any food preparation to give it an "exotic" essence. They are commonly used in sauces, ice creams, marinades, coulis, in combination with a seafood item, chutneys (when green and under-ripe), salsa, relishes, jam, in curry dishes, pickled, candied, frozen, fresh, dried, or the most commonly used method straight out of the hand.

HINT:
Store close to 50 degrees for up to 2 weeks. If you buy under-ripe mangos, place them in a paper bag with a banana for a day or two and they will be perfect.

◇ Common availability of Mangos...
Haden...July-October (Florida)
Keitt...May-September (Florida)
Kent...January-Feburary and June-August (worldwide)
Tommy Atkins....October-August (worldwide)
Van Dyke...June-July (worldwide)

1 cup of raw mango equals 107 calories and will provide 76% of your vitamin C for the day.

As you see, availability can be year-round depending on where mangos are being harvested. The production leaders worldwide are: Mexico, leading with almost 90 percent of all exports, then Peru, Venezuela, Brazil and Ecuador all come in about the same in yearly production levels.

Culinary uses

NEW WORLD SQUASH~Calabaza

The Mayans and Aztecs were the first to use this pumpkin-like squash. It traveled well with the earliest settlers of Florida. The Spanish and English settlers used this squash as well as the West Indians. Thus, English settlers deemed it the "West Indian Squash".

Remove the skin and you will find the flesh has a fine-grained texture that lends itself to many dishes. It could be used in soups, as a condiment for salads, vegetable stir-fries, braised in meat dishes, chopped for fritters and used in cakes. It can be pureed, chopped, stewed, sauteed, boiled or used the same way our American pumpkin is used.

To Use:
Its flesh is bright yellow with edible seeds, that most times are toasted for snacking or used for pestos. Choose tight-fleshed squash and don't worry if they are too large, they normally keep for months. You can also cook, puree and freeze the flesh for up to a year. This product is handy in "Spa" cuisine; it has a high fiber content with relatively few calories.

This can make an excellent substitute for Hubbard, Acorn, Butternut squashes or our North American pumpkin.

1 cup contains about 35 calories.

Available most of the year with Florida being the main supplier throughout the world.

Culinary uses

PASSION FRUIT, Nature's own palate cleanser

This fruit was discovered by missionaries in Brazil. Its name came from its flower which is produced by the plant before fruiting: a beautiful purple color, with a stamen that is white with many smaller stamen surrounding the larger, central one. It was thought the flower resembled the crucifixion of Christ with the Apostles surrounding him.

The passionfruit is very colorful, in purple, yellow, green with a red/pink hue and orange outer shells. The taste of the tropics is unsurpassed within its shell. Most of these different varieties grow in South Florida, but the most common are the purple and yellow varieties. The Maypop, a family member, has grown in Florida since the time of Columbus. Growers are working to produce a variety that is sweeter than the original. The Jamaican variety has a sweet-tart flavor.

To Use:
Its extraordinary scent lends itself well to chicken dishes, marinades and makes a great seasoning ingredient. It can also be used in pies, drinks, ices, mousses, souffles, tarts, vinegar, marinades and sauces. Although it has a tough outer shell (wrinkled looking when ripe and ready to use), this product couldn't be easier to use. Just split in two and scoop out its pulp. Heat a little to facilitate seed removal, with sugar to ease its acidity.

Passionfruit has about 90 calories per 3.5 oz. of pulp. The pulp is also very high in vitamins A, C and is a good source for potassium.

Available May through July in Florida.

Culinary uses

SWAMP CABBAGE, heart of Palm

Heart of palm is Florida's best kept secret. This is a product that should always be use fresh and has no reasonable substitute. Any canned or imported product doesn't have the bite or freshness of a palm straight from the field, although fresh is a harder product to find and use, the results are worth every effort.

In the Lake Okeechobee region of Florida, this product is referred to as the "poor man's cauliflower" because of its accessibility. It costs less than cauliflower, and can be used in many of the same recipes. There is even a central Florida food festival dedicated to this product. The Sable Palm grows like a weed and is so plentiful, it is hard to go anywhere in most of Florida without seeing one.

The Sable Palm is the best example of a true indigenous staple of South Florida's culinary history. It has been used by countless generations of native South Florida Indians and I believe with a little experimentation, it can be a part of a modern larder also.

To Use:
Early Florida pioneers used them along with black-eyed peas for their vegetables on the dinner plate. "True Southerners" in central Florida use it in an ice cream and in a mayonnaise salad. In the Keys it is made into a fritter mixed with fruits and deep fried. A Florida "Cracker" presentation of this product comes from a Civil War town along the West Coast that requires the swamp cabbage to be tossed with various tropical fruits and a light sherbet dressing. When using this product, slice thinly and toss into an acidic water solution so it doesn't turn brown, then add into various preparations.

1 cup has 41 calories and contains 25 % of your daily requirement of iron.

Available year round.

Culinary uses

TAMARIND

This product, is not native to South Florida, but grows with regularity. It was brought to us from Africa by the earliest traders to the West Indies. The Tamarind tree is quite tall and grows as wild as a weed in the Redlands. Tamarind pods are collected as they fall from the tree, or as one might collect olives-by spreading out a bed sheet and shaking them off smaller trees.

To Use:
After being gathered, they are manipulated into many forms. The first and most simple is candy, made with just the addition of palm sugar to its pulp. The people of the Orient use this product as a substitute for a sour taste in any recipe that might have originally called for lime or vinegar.

The pod shell is removed and the pulp is used in various ways depending on cultural preferences. Besides being the main ingredient in Worchestire Sauce, it is also used in Latin salsa, Oriental soups, tenderizers, and West Indian curry dishes. It can be found in dry packaged form, frozen concentrate and fresh in shell. The pulp is easily removed when soaked in warm water first.

1 oz. of tamarind has 67 calories.

Available all year, found in Latin and Caribbean grocers.

Culinary uses

UGLIFRUIT

The Uglifruit is a fruit from Jamaica that I have had the pleasure to know for some time. Its fantastic taste encourages the mind to wonder about all of its possible recipe combinations. Uglifruit is a cross between the Mandarin and Seville oranges, with grapefruit with limited bitterness. You will be pleased with the waste factor as well-considering the size of the fruit, its usable flesh is of great proportion.

The wrinkled, loose fitting skin (its namesake) is easily removed to reveal a sweet orange colored flesh that has the taste-variance of a grapefruit. The smaller the fruit, the more tangy the flavor. The zest can be used in pesto, compotes, and as a base to gremolata. The fruit is easily removed and sectioned for use in salads, salad dressings, marinades, used with poultry (especially duck), mousses, cakes, puddings, cold souffles, beurre blancs, fruit compotes, coulis-grettes and drinks.

To use:
As you would any citrus fruit.

Available January through April.

Bouchee's
-little Mouthfuls-

S INTENSELY FLAVORED~
M
A SMALLER PORTIONS ARE
L A MAJOR PART OF THE
L SOUTH FLORIDA DINING
EXPERIENCE.

IT IS BETTER TO USE A
LITTLE OF SOMETHING
INTENSE!

B
i
t
e
s

Breadfruit Soup

Serves: 6

A hearty soup served with fried slices of breadfruit. Use the crisp pieces as a garnish or float atop the soup and use as a raft to hold pieces of grilled shrimp and dill sprigs

Ingredients:

2	cups	Breadfruit, save 6 slices for a garnish-see notes
1	tbs.	Oil
As needed		Salt and pepper, 5:1 ratio
1	each	Onion, chopped
2	each	Garlic, cloves, crushed
1/2	each	Scotch Bonnet pepper, finely chopped
1	cup	Chicken stock (or seafood stock)
1/4	cup	White wine
3	oz.	Heavy cream
1/4	teas.	Nutmeg
2	tbs.	Chives, chopped

Instructions:

Cut the skin off the breadfruit and then cut into chunks to cook easier. Coat in oil to prevent browning. Boil until they soften like potatoes-for mashing. Saute the garlic, onion and add the breadfruit after they turn translucent. Add the stock, wine and Scotch bonnet chili. Cook about 25 minutes until everything is soft. Grind to a fine puree with an immersible blender. Add cream to soften the puree, season again to taste. Garnish with chopped chives and just a little nutmeg dust.

Notes:

For snacking:
After slicing off the breadfruits skin, cut a wedge, less than the thickness of a pencil, from the globe. Deep fry until crisp. Season with salt and pepper.

St Barts Crab Cake

Serves: 4

This recipe is one of my all-time favorites. Everyone loves it because the cakes have no bread filler. To accomplish this recipe, it has to be done just so. This a multiple-stage recipe, start the day before for best results. The crabcakes should be frozen the day before so they don't fall apart.

Ingredients:

8	oz.	Lump crabmeat
8	oz.	Jumbo-lump crabmeat
2	oz.	Bell peppers, tricolored, diced
2	oz.	Onions, chopped
3	oz.	Mango, chopped fine
1/2	oz.	Pickled ginger, finely chopped
3	tbs.	Cilantro, leaves only, chopped
4	each	Egg whites
1	tbs.	Zanathan gum (found in specialty health food stores)
10	oz.	Passionfruit sauce, see recipe page 108
2	tbs.	Stone ground mustard
As needed		Oil, shallow for frying
2	bunch	Broccolini, blanched salted water, cool in ice water
1	bunch	Pencil asparagus, blanched in salted water, cool again

Breading station:

1 1/2	cups	Panko bread crumbs (found in specialty markets)
1/2	cup	Pecan nuts, toasted in a 325 degree oven for then minutes, then crushed in a food processor
1	cup	Dredging flour, seasoned with salt and pepper
2	cups	Milk, with 4 whole beaten eggs added to make the *wash*

Second half:

2	cups	Peruvian purple potatoes, chopped in half or thirds
As needed		Oil, for sauteing
As needed		Salt and pepper
1.4	cup	Scallions, chopped
2	tbs.	Red bell peppers, diced small

Garnish:

1	head	Baby Frisse, leaves
1	small	Beet, peel, cut with a spiral cutter, place in cool water, drain before using (you could use a carrot instead of the beet)
2	tbs.	Micro herbs (found in your local gourmet grocery)
1/5	bag	Angelhair pasta
As needed		Fry oil, from above, in a deeper pot

Directions:

(This can be done the day before) Toss all the veggie and mango ingredients together. Place the next three ingredients into a food processor and grind them into a slurry. Add the slurry to the veggie mix. Add the crab meats to the mix, tossing very gently so you don't break the jumbo lump crab. Divide the mix up into 4 cakes, form into patties using a (3 inch) ring mold, freeze to harden

con't after pictures

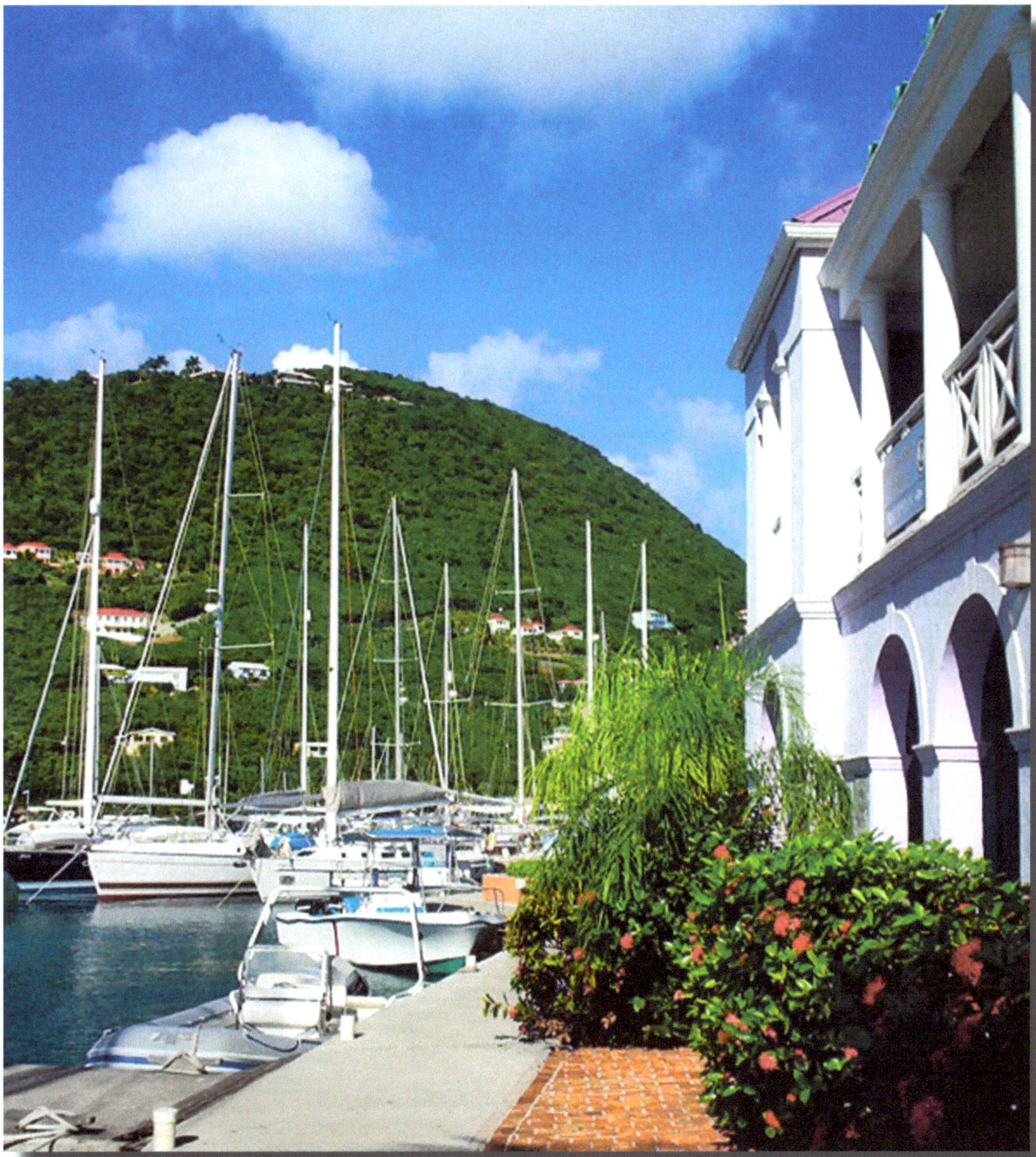

Sailing port in the British Virgin Islands.
Once thought to be Black Beard's hideout.
A place for modern day...

Pirates!

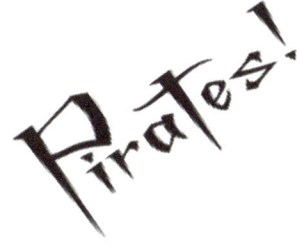

BOCHEES

SO THEY ARE EASIER TO BREAD. REMOVE FROM FREEZER. SET UP BREADING STATION (FLOUR, MILK WASH AND PANKO/NUT MIX). DIP THE FROZEN CAKES INTO FLOUR, THEN MILK WASH (DRAINING EXCESS) AND THEN INTO PANKO CRUMBS MIXED WITH THE GROUND NUTS. COVER CAKES ON ALL SIDES WITH THE MIX. LAY OUT ONTO A SHEET PAN AND FREEZE COMPLETELY, UNTIL YOU ARE READY TO COOK.

NEXT:

FRY THE FROZEN CAKES IN HOT OIL UNTIL THE CRUST IS BROWN, COOKING ABOUT THREE MINUTES PER SIDE OF THE CRABCAKE. PLACE ON A COOKIE TRAY AND FINISH COOKING IN A 350 DEGREE PREHEATED OVEN UNTIL CENTER IS HOT - ABOUT 8 MINUTES.

NEXT STEP:

(THIS CAN BE DONE THE DAY BEFORE) PLACE THE POTATOES IN A POT OF HEAVILY SALTED WATER AND BOIL UNTIL YOU CAN STICK A FORK IN THEM. DRAIN, DRY AND WHEN READY TO SERVE; TOSS IN THE HOT OIL LEFT OVER FROM THE COOKING OF THE CRAB AND SAUTE THE POTATOES. SEASON, TOSS WITH THE OTHER VEGGIE GARNISHMENTS. FORM INTO CIRCLES - USING THE SAME SIZE RING MOLD AS THE CRABCAKE - ON THE CENTER OF EACH PLATE. PRESSING DOWN ON THE COOKED POTATOES TO FORM A CAKE.

(VEGGIES) IN BOILING SALTED WATER, BLANCH THE BROCCOLINI AND ASPARAGUS, SEPARATELY. AS THE DARK GREEN TURNS TO A BRIGHT GREEN, REMOVE AND PLACE IN A COLD ICE WATER BATH TO STOP THE COOKING PROCESS AND SET THE COLOR OF THE VEGGIES. DRAIN WELL WHEN YOU ARE READY TO PLATE EVERYTHING. SAUTE TO WARM UP AGAIN. SEASON AND PLACE ATOP THE POTATOES - AS SEEN IN THE PICTURE.

GARNISH:

IN A DEEP POT, ENOUGH TO SUBMERGE A LADLE, COOK THE ANGELHAIR GARNISH. SUBMERGE A DRY SOUP LADLE INTO HOT OIL. PUSH THE ANGELHAIR INTO THE BOWL OF THE LADLE, LETTING THE NOODLES SOFTEN EVER SO SOFTLY AS YOU PUSH THE STRAIGHT NOODLES BEGIN TO HOOK. THEN WHILE THEY ARE STILL TWISTING AND HOOKING JUST DROP WHATEVER IS IN YOUR HAND INTO THE OIL. LET COOK THERE FOR THREE MINUTES UNTIL SLIGHTLY BROWN. REMOVE AND DRAIN EXCESS OIL. SEASON THE HOT FRIED NOODLES WITH SALT AND PEPPER. COOL. AND THEN PLACE INTO THE CRABCAKE - LIKE IN THE PICTURE. JUST SPEAR THE NOODLES INTO THE SOFT CAKE. PLACE THE SPIRAL BEETS INTERLACED WITH BABY FRISSE AND MICRO-HERBS ATOP THE CRABCAKE.

SAUCE:

GENTLY MIX THE PASSIONFRUIT SAUCE WITH AND ADDITION OF "POMMERY" MUSTARD. JUST SWIRL THE MUSTARD INTO THE PASSIONFRUIT SAUCE. IT WILL MIX INTO THE SAUCE AND GIVE A TOTALLY DIFFERENT LOOK TO THE COLOR. DRIZZLE ONTO THE PLATE (AFTER THE CRABCAKE IS SET ONTO THE POTATO MELANGE) SURROUNDING THE CAKECAKE STACK.

"Not your Mother's" Calamari

SERVES: 6

The title says it all. From the go, this recipe is different. The cornmeal sets a crunch that is unexpected, The rice flour is a soft textured flour that is so different than wheat flour, I had to include this recipe in my book.

INGREDIENTS:

3	LB.	Calamari, tubes only (sliced into 1/2 inch rings)
1	BOTTLE	Jamaican beer
As needed		Milk wash (1 cup half and half, and 1 egg)
1	LB	Rice flour, found in Asian markets
1/2	LB.	Cornmeal, fine
As needed		Spikes seasoning (for the flours)
Garni		Use the garnishes from previous recipe

DIRECTIONS:

Toss the flour and cornmeal together and season. Cut the calamari into rings. Place in beer overnight. Drain and then toss into seasoned flour, shake off excess, dip into milk wash, and then into the cornmeal-rice flour blend again. Fry as usual removing before the rings become too crisp. You want them just cooked past the raw state.

TO USE:

What I like to do is toss the cooked calamari in one of the sauces before serving. This means you have to be ready to serve right away because the calamari will become soggy if they rest too long before eating.

To do this step...thin the sauce recipe slightly (when needed with an appropriate white wine or fruit juice). Place the calamari in a bowl large enough for tossing. Drizzle a little of the sauce over the rings. Toss gently so the crust doesn't break. Place in a large martini glass and serve. Garnish with some fresh chopped cilantro and fried pasta noddles as a garnish to create even more height.

FOR DIPS:

Orange-maple-allspice sauce, see recipe on page 106
Fire-Spice Papaya BBQ sauce, see recipe on page 107

CRITTER FRITTERS
SERVES: 10

'Gator taste of freshwater Bass crossed with pork. Meat is very lean with only 3 percent fat. An excellent "Low-fat" entree recipe.

INGREDIENTS:

2	LBS.	Alligator tail, thinly sliced & slightly pounded
2	FRUIT	Lemon, juice
As needed		Salt
1/2	CUP	Cajun-blackening spice blend, see recipe
As needed		Vegetable oil

INSTRUCTIONS:

Season with lemon juice and salt. Let marinate three minutes. Shake off liquid, dredge in creole spice. Shake off excess, saute quickly in oil. Drain. Serve.

What really goes well with this is a sassy chipotle passionfruit "coulisgrette" on page 74 - as a dipping sauce.

LOBSTER AND WILD MUSHROOM FILO ROLLS
SERVES: 6

1	LB.	Caribbean lobster tailmeat, cooked, (from a 2 1/2 lb. lobster)
2	OZ.	Olive oil
1	OZ.	Shallots, chopped roughly
6	OZ.	Shiitaki mushrooms, large julienne slices
2	OZ.	Snow peas, julienned
2	OZ.	Red onions, julienned
1	CUP	Spinach, chiffonade
4	EACH	Basil leaves, chiffonade
2	OZ.	Passionfruit sauce, see page 108
As needed		Salt and pepper, 5:1 ratio
2	TBS.	Butter, room temperature
10-12	EACH	Filo dough sheets
As needed		Garnishing sauces, see below

DIRECTIONS:

Saute the veggies with the oil in the order they are listed in the recipe. Make sure they still have a crunch, add the spinach and basil, toss, remove from heat and cool. Add the coulis-grette when cool and decoratively garnish the plate with the sauce.

CON'T NEXT PAGE

Heat oven to 375 degrees. Lay out the filo on a dry surface. Butter 3 sheets of filo and lay out in layers using softened butter in between each sheet. Lay the lobster slices on the top sheet, spread the veggie mix over it. Fold in the ends of the filo dough and roll into a tube. Seal the last edge with a little more butter and place sealed side down on a cookie sheet. Spread a little more butter over top of the filo dough roll. Bake about 11 minutes until the filo is just tan. Remove, when cool enough to handle, slice on bias and place decoratively on a plate. Garnish with a small micro greens salad or fresh herbs.

Garnishing sauce:

Add a spot of the sprouted mustard seed sauce (see page 105 under the presentation on the plate). Then, using the cherimoya beurre blanc (see page 100) and spicy red curry guava glaze (on page 103). Drizzle all around the presentation.

This recipe is one you might find in the French Caribbean islands.
With the exotic tastes of passionfruit and lobster
it is a dish you will want to make for all your special
occasion dinners.

Lobster and Wild Mushroom Filo Rolls on page 44-45

A VIEW FROM MY HOME IN THE CARIBBEAN

L
I
F
E

Curry grilled Shrimp
see page 50

Spicy glazed Mango

Serves: 4

Ingredients:

3	TBS.	Orange juice
3	TBS.	Honey, orange blossom
2	TEAS.	Cumin, powder
1	TEAS.	Jalopeno, finely chopped
2	EACH	Mangos

Instructions:

Mix the first five ingredients together in a stainless steel pot and reduce to a light syrup over high heat.

Cut off the Mango's skin. Slice down each side of the pit taking off two dome shaped pieces. Slice these pieces into slivers crosswise through each half about 1/8 of an inch thick. Drop these slices into the glaze for just a second and remove.

To Use: Place on plate as an accompaniment to any grilled seafood or poultry item.

Toasty crispy Mango

Serves: 4

Ingredients:

2	EACH	Mangos, sliced thin
1/3	CUP	Flour
1	PINCH	Salt
1	TEAS.	Sugar
1	EACH	Egg
1/2	CUP	Coconut milk, use canned for simplicity
3/4	CUP	Coconut, grated
As needed		Grapeseed oil, or peanut oil

Con't on next page....

Hints:

If possible, use the Tommy Atkins mango for this procedure

INSTRUCTIONS:
SEASON FLOUR WITH THE SALT AND SUGAR. LIGHTLY DREDGE THE SLICES OF MANGO IN FLOUR AND THEN INTO THE BATTER OF EGG AND COCONUT MILK. SHAKE OFF A LITTLE OF THE JUICY BATTER AND DROP INTO THE COCONUT. PAT THE SLICES LIGHTLY SO THE FLAKES STAY ON. HAVE THE OIL IN A NON-STICK SKILLET. QUICKLY MOVE THE SLICES OF MANGO FROM THE COCONUT TO THE SAUTE PAN AND SEAR-CRISPY ON ONE SIDE AND GENTLY FLIP WITH A SMALL SPATULA AND CRISP AGAIN. WHEN THE OTHER SIDE IS CARAMELIZED LIFT UP AND DRAIN SLIGHTLY.

THIS A GREAT RECIPE FOR THE FOLLOWING...

> BANANA BASS ON PAGE 123
> SEABASS WITH CHIMI-CHURRI ON PAGE 130
> PEPPER-SPIKED MAKO ON PAGE 137

STONE CRAB AND CALABAZA FRITTERS

SERVES: 6

MAKE THE RECIPE FOR CURRY YOGURT DRESSING AND USE AS A DIPPING SAUCE. STONE CRAB, A FAVORITE SOUTH FLORIDA TREAT MAKES THIS SOMETHING YOUR GUEST WILL REMEMBER. ASK YOUR FISHMONGER FOR CRAB ALREADY OUT OF THE SHELL. LARGE CRAB HOUSES ALWAYS HAVE BROKEN LEGS THEY SPLIT AND PACK THE MEAT FOR SALADS AND APPETIZERS.

INGREDIENTS:

1 1/2	LBS.	CALABAZA, BLANCHED UNTIL SOFT
1/2	LB.	STONE CRAB MEAT, WELL DRAINED
3/4	CUP	WHOLE WHEAT FLOUR
1/4	CUP	HONEY, ORANGE BLOSSOM
1	TEAS.	BAKING POWDER, OR TRY 1 PKG. OF DRY YEAST
AS NEEDED		SALT AND PEPPER, 5:1 RATIO
2	EACH	EGGS, SEPARATED
AS NEEDED		PEANUT OIL
AS NEEDED		CURRY YOGURT DRESSING, SEE RECIPE ON PAGE 75

INSTRUCTIONS:
SEPARATE WHITES FROM YOLKS. WHIP WHITES STIFF. CUT THE BLANCHED AND COOKED-SOFT CALABAZA INTO A SMALL DICE. MIX THE DRY INGREDIENTS TOGETHER. ADD TO THE YOLKS. ADD THE CALABAZA AND CRABMEAT TO THE YOLKS AND THEN STIR IN THE FLOUR MIXTURE, FOLD IN WHITES. FORM MIXTURE INTO 1 1/2 INCH BALLS AND DROP INTO OIL. COOK ABOUT THREE MINUTES. TEST ONE BY BREAKING IT OPEN TO SEE IF THE INSIDE IS COOKED-DRY. DRAIN, SERVE HOT.

Curry grilled Shrimp with Pineapple salsa

Serves: 4

Ingredients:

16	each	Shrimp, under 7 to a pound, peeled and deveined
1 1/2	tbs.	Curry spice (use the better quality brands)
2	cup	Pineapple salsa (see papaya salsa recipe below using pineapple)
As needed		Uglifruit "coulisgrette" (see hints)
As needed		Wood chips, soaked

Instructions:
Soak wood chips 20 minutes. After the chips are tossed on the coals, pat some spice onto shrimp and place onto oiled grill. Close the lid and let cook for about 8 minutes. Make the salsa, substituting the pineapple instead of papaya. Place the shrimp on top of the salsa in the center of the plate. Glaze lightly with the coulisgrette.

Hints: Use the Ugli-fruit "coulisgrette" recipe on page 74 to glaze the shrimp after cooking.

Papaya Salsa

Serves: 10

Ingredients:

1	(3 lbs.)	Papaya, diced
2	each	Scotch bonnet, finely chopped
1	each	Banana chili pepper, diced
2	each	Lime, juice
2	tbs.	Red bell pepper, finely diced
1 1/2	tbs.	Cilantro, chopped
2	tbs.	Red onion, diced
2	tbs.	Olive oil

Instructions:
Cut all the fruit and veggies the same sized dice. Place in non-reactive bowl. Sprinkle with the Lime juice. Toss lightly. Fold in the cilantro and oil. Let rest just a few minutes. Use as needed.

Hints: This salsa can be changed easily by substituting an equal amount of any other tropical fruits like: starfruit, pineapple, mango, mamey, etc....

Portabella-St. John's crab sandwich

Serves: 5

The title "sandwich" is kind of misleading. It is actually "stuffed" like an ice cream sandwich.

Ingredients:

5	each	Large Portabella mushrooms, clean gills, slice in half, horizontally
25	each	Asparagus pencil-thin, blanched
2	each	Garlic, chopped
2	oz.	Extra-virgin olive oil
1/2	teas.	Salt and pepper, 5:1 ratio
1	tbs.	Olive oil
2	tbs.	Shallots, fine
1/2	each	Key lime
1	lb.	Blue crab meat, cleaned well
3	tbs.	Red bell pepper, diamond cuts
1	tbs.	Cilantro, chopped
5	oz.	Opal basil Viniaigrette (see page 73)

Instructions:

Rub mushrooms with oil and seasonings, let sit 3 hours in refrigerator. Heat grill and brush with oil. Carefully cook the mushrooms, making sure they are cooked all the way through, then cool and slice horizontally.

Quickly saute the shallots. Add the crab and toss rapidly. Season. Garnish with the peppers and cilantro. Place asparagus on plate at; 1:30, 4:00, 7:00, 9:00, 11:00 radiating outward from the center of the plate. Place the bottom halves of the mushrooms atop the center of the asparagus ends. Fill with equal portions of the crabmeat mixture. Top with other portion of the mushroom cap.

Garnish plate with whole cilantro leaves and diamond cuts of red and yellow bell peppers. Sprinkle a little cracked black pepper over entire plate.

> The Portabella gets softer as it cooks.
> When it gives to pressure like
> a ripe persimmon, when it is ready.

GROUND-NUT CRUSTED GOAT'S CHEESE

SERVES: 4

"TURTLE-CREEK" GOAT CHEESE IS A LOCALLY PRODUCED FAVORITE.

INGREDIENTS:

12	OZ.	GOAT CHEESE
4	OZ.	LICHEES, SHELLED, DE-SEEDED
6	OZ.	PEANUTS OR CASHEWS
1/3	CUP	FLOUR, SEASONED
AS NEEDED		EGGWASH
AS NEEDED		FRYING OIL
4	OZ.	COOKED BLACK BEANS
1/2	EACH	MAMEY SAPOTE, DICED
1/3	EACH	PAPAYA, DICED
1/3	EACH	RED BELL PEPPER, DICED
1	EACH	KEY LIME, JUICE
1	OZ.	OLIVE OIL
2	TBS.	CILANTRO
1/2	EACH	HABENERO PEPPER, FINELY DICED
1	EACH	SUGAR APPLE, OVER-RIPE, PEELED, DICED
8	EACH	KEY LIMES, JUICE (EQUALS 8 TBS.)
1/3	TEAS.	SALT
2	OZ.	EXTRA-VIRGIN OLIVE OIL
AS NEEDED		CANE SYRUP, FOUND AT SPECIALTY GROCERS.
AS NEEDED		TABASCO SAUCE
3	EACH	VELVET APPLES, SLICED FOR GARNISH

INSTRUCTIONS:

MIX THE GOAT CHEESE WITH THE CHOPPED LICHEES. MOLD INTO A CYLINDER AND CUT INTO WHEELS (8). FREEZE SLIGHTLY TO MAKE IT EASIER TO MANAGE. CRUSH THE PEANUTS IN A FOOD PROCESSOR. SEASON. ROLL THE CHEESE IN A LITTLE FLOUR, THEN EGGWASH AND THEN INTO THE PEANUTS. SAUTE QUICKLY. DRAIN ON ABSORBENT TOWELS. KEEP WARM.

TO MAKE SALSA: MIX THE NEXT 8 INGREDIENTS QUICKLY AND PLATE.

TO MAKE SAUCE: PUREE THE SUGAR APPLE WITH THE NEXT 3 INGREDIENTS IN A CUISINART. ADD THE OIL SLOWLY. FLAVOR AS NEEDED WITH THE TABASCO AND SYRUP. LAY THE SLICED APPLES AROUND EDGE OF PLATE. PLACE SALSA IN CENTER OF PLATE IN A STACK. TOP WITH TWO DISKS OF CHEESE. NAPPE THE PLATE AT 6:00 WITH COULISGRETTE.

Vegan Truffles

SERVES: 6

Maybe this is a mis-named menu item, but you'll catch my drift. Use these dipping sauces such as Avocado-Yogurt dressing, Mango Mayo or the Curry Yogurt dip for a unique taste from South Florida.

INGREDIENTS:

1	LB.	Split peas, soaked overnight
2	EACH	Garlic cloves, crushed
1	TEAS.	Saffron powder, found in Latin markets
1/4	TEAS.	Baking powder
2	TBS.	Flour
1 1/2	TEAS.	Salt
1	TBS.	Jalapenos, finely chopped
2	TBS.	Red bell peppers, diced
4	TBS.	Green bell peppers, diced
As needed		Oil for frying

HINTS:
For something a little different, try adding chiffonade of mint, basil or thyme.

INSTRUCTIONS:

Drain the peas. Dry and crush the first two ingredients in a food processor, then place in a mixing bowl and stir in the rest of the ingredients. This is where you can add chiffonade of herbs or even chunks of crabmeat. Drain, and then hold warm. Dip in the sauces listed above.

Salads

Exciting, Playful foods~
Cooling and refreshing,
Tropical salads are natural coolants.

The Redlands

A cookbook is a tool people use to visit far off places and taste cuisines from all over the world. In the past to experience exotic tropical tastes you would have had to get on an airplane and fly to the Caribbean. This has all changed. For the past handful of decades, South Florida has been growing exotic tropical food. This growing region, known as the Redlands, gives us all the perfect opportunity to experience an airmail destination cuisine without boarding a jet.

The Redlands traditionally grows plant species from across the exotic tropical regions of the world. It is like a transplanted Garden of Eden. The Redlands is a smaller version of California's Napa Valley. Here we are fortunate enough to enjoy these tropical extravagances fresh from the farm. This area has become the focal point for the exotic food used in this book. It is an agricultural wonderland, existing a few miles from major traffic tie ups and skyscrapers of steel and glass.

Before Hurricane Andrew destroyed South Florida, we produced more tropical and exotic food than anywhere else in the United States. **The encyclopedic variety of tropical products that are grown here is overwhelming.** South Florida also produces more than a dozen kinds of bananas, 250 different mangos and more than 25 other varieties of "rare" and exotic fruit.

What all these growers realize is that South Florida, being sub-tropical, rarely if ever, does it freeze. This condition, along with better than average rainfall and high humidity, makes south Florida an ideal location to grow these exotic tropical treasures. South Florida is the only place in our nation with these conditions. Since 1926, South Florida has been an optimal growing area for this food category and this is the reason why we will be touting South Florida as America's newest "Napa Valley". In the future South Florida will be the place where America looks for its culinary amusement.

America's population is becoming more and more culturally ethnic. South Florida's newest residents originate from many countries lying within the equatorial longitudes of the world. Each of these transplanted cultures bring with them their own individual culinary heritage.

When one travels the roads of the Redlands mango, papaya and tamarind trees are seen everywhere. The spirit and pride of the people who grow these products is contagious. After interviewing a few of these exotic fruit growers, I find myself spending a lot more time with new friends, all the while witnessing the birth of a new horizon for the food service industry.

The Morning Market

As you pass over the last bridge that takes you to your" Kingdom du Jour", the sun is almost blinding as it peaks across the crest of the horizon. Your eyes adjust quickly because you have already had the lights from the morning produce market burning your retinas since five o'clock. Working as a chef on the New American Riviera, you gather with other chefs at the morning market at least twice a week to inspect the products that will go into recipes your Mother never would have thought of.

Our day begins as the sun warms the early morning mist. It starts off early with a gaggle of chefs going from one produce vendor to another, checking provisions for quality and prices. After several stops, the pace of their buying quickens. Comparing prices from one vendor to another, you realize the bargains that are right in front of you and hurry the sale. Many of these merchants are eager to push the sale of these products from their refrigerators so they can make room for the next restock from the Redlands.

Touring this areas's warehouse-size, refrigerated produce storage facilities, you find that they are always stocked with tropical provisions. Food is stacked on pallets by forklifts, and racked into shelving like five story bunk beds. The forklifts run in and out of the refrigerators like semi-trucks that crush the nearby freeways. While these produce warehouses are as modern as the metropolis just over the bridge, there are also local growers hawking backyard grown products lining the streets. This is where a Macy's bargain basement pricing strategy reigns supreme.

The street vendors have produce you'll have to pick over - like when your Mother dragged you over to the Macy's sale rack. Backyard growers have been busy on these streets since the beginning of Miami's history. South Floridians have always had an natural urge and pride to show off (and sell) their backyard harvests. You can see it and hear it in everything they do. Sometimes you know which stand to buy from just by looking at the care in which the produce is stacked in the bins.

We are lucky today-chefs can always find quality products with our harvesting acreage so close by, freshness is never a question. The products finding their way to the market streets are sometimes only hours old from these nearby farms.

After making your way through these city streets, the sky is just turning a pale blue, when a rain shower begins and a cloudy mist of humidity starts to rise from the already sweltering asphalt streets. Even at this time of the day, one can feel the heat of the tropics. The people at the market carry on as usual.

It is just another muggy day in the Magic-city.

Spa Veggy Antipasto

Serves: 30

"Spa" in the title represents "spa cuisine" usually meaning that the total fat content of this recipe is below 30 percent for the recipe's total calorie count. This recipe is great to take to those summertime company picnics and family outings.

Ingredients:

2	lbs.	Yellow tomatoes, chopped
5	lbs.	Florida eggplant, diced
1	lbs.	Red onion, diced
2	lbs.	Field mushrooms, quartered
2	each	Assorted peppers, julienned
1	each	Cauliflower florets
5	each	Celery stalks, bias cut
2	tbs.	Garlic, chopped
2	oz.	Olive oil
1	cup	Tomato paste
1	cup	Neutral stock
1/2	cup	Rice wine vinegar
1	cup	Black olives, sliced
1	cup	Green olives, sliced
To taste		Oregano, salt, pepper, sugar

Hints: This is great for something completely different.

Instructions:

Gently sweat (cook over a low heat) summer's favorite veggies...yellow tomato, eggplant, and mushrooms and other veggies in olive oil starting with the garlic. Add the paste after the veggies are half cooked. Stirring it into the mixture. Let the paste flavor the veggies for three minutes.

Add the rest of the ingredients and cook until veggies are tender. Add the liquids and the other flavoring ingredients.

Remove from heat, let cool and refrigerate overnight. Serve as a salad cold with sandwiches or as a side dish for cold entrees.

Florida Bliss Potato salad

Serves: 25

Another great salad that we make in abundance for big family outings. Use as a side dish for roasted pork or spicy main meal recipes.

Ingredients:

5	LBS.	Bliss potatoes, halved, skin-on, steamed soft
1	LBS.	Assorted sweet bell peppers, julienne
1	LBS.	Red onions, julienne
1/2	BUNCH	Scallions, cut on the bias
1/4	CUP	Chives, snipped on the bias
1	EACH	Scotch bonnet pepper, diced
2	EACH	Orange, segmented
2	TBS.	Habenero pepper vinegar
2	EACH	Lime juice
1/2	CUP	Orange juice, concentrate
2	TEAS.	Chili powder
1	EACH	Scotch bonnet, finely diced
1	CUP	Rice wine vinegar
1	CUP	Olive oil

Hints:

This recipe is the one you will take to the company picnic every year

Instructions:

Make the dressing with the last 7 ingredients. Season if necessary. Toss the peppers, onions and orange segment together. Add the dressing and toss. Pour this over the potatoes, lightly toss. Place in serving bowl and garnish with more julienne peppers and orange segments.

Florida grows an abundance of foods you would never expect from a southern state. Red bliss potatoes are just one of those food products.

Spicy Wasabi Cucumbers

Serves: 8

A great recipe to pair with sesame seared tuna steaks

Ingredients:

2	each	Florida cucumbers
2	tbs.	Rice wine vinegar
1	teas.	Sesame oil
1 1/2	teas.	Wasabi
As needed		Habenero pepper sauce
1	each	Scallion, bias cut
1	tbs.	White & black sesame seeds

Instructions:

Slice cucumbers and season with salt and pepper. Let drain for 3 minutes. Mix the rest of the ingredients for the dressing. Toss both batches of ingredients and save until needed. Serve within one hour.

Hints: Place the sliced cuccumber like a necklace around the protein portion of the entree. These tastes will dance on your tongue.

Green Papaya Kimchee

Serves: 10-12

Ingredients:

1	cup	Green papaya (see hints)
1	cup	Napa cabbage, shredded
1/2	cup	Snow peas, julienne
2	oz.	Red onion, julienne
2	oz.	Red bell pepper, julienne
7	each	Garlic, sliced thinly
1/4	cup	Carrot, julienne
4	oz.	Pineapple, julienne
2	tbs.	Cilantro, chopped
1	teas.	Sriracha sauce, *more if you like it spicy*
1	teas.	Sesame oil
1 1/2	tbs.	Salt
2	teas.	Ginger, crushed finely
1/3	cup	Scallions, sliced thinly on a bias

Con't...next page

Hints: Green papaya is a specialty product. You will really have to look around for a purveyor willing to stock a product like this.

INSTRUCTIONS:
Cut the green papaya (no skin or seeds) and the nappa cabbage finely. Season heavily with kosher salt. Let drain in a colander for just over an hour. Add the rest of the ingredients starting with the rest of the veggies. Add the flavorings and mix well. Let drain again for about an hour. Place in plastic or non-reactive container and refrigerate until you need to use it.

This recipe goes well with outdoor picnic meals. It can set out at room temperature for long periods of time without a problem.

This recipe pairs well with other bold flavored foods or recipes that have protein elements that are rich in flavor. It also goes perfectly with rich tasting fish filets (see notes in seafood section about how to tell which fish are higher in flavor). Use as a garnishing salad that might be atop seafood dishes or placed into fried tortilla cups and placed along side of the protein portion of the entree.

Use with strong flavored dishes you will find in this book like:
Spicy guava BBQ ribs, on page 153
South Florida Po-Poo platter, on page 152
Fire-roasted turkey loin, on page 155

Jicama-Melon salsa

Serves: 4
Use for garnishing seafood plates to ad an extra element of flavor for the entree.

Ingredients:
1	each	Mango
2	each	Key lime juice
1	each	Scotch bonnet pepper
3	tbs.	Red bell pepper, chopped
1/2	cup	Cantaloupe, chopped
1/2	cup	Honeydew, chopped
1/2	cup	Jicama, julienned
2	tbs.	Cilantro
1	tbs.	Olive oil
As needed		Salt and pepper

Instructions:
Peel mango and chop in cuisinart with the lime juice and the scotch bonnet. Place in a bowl and toss in the rest of the ingredients. Toss all well to coat. Season if needed.

Black Bean, Heart of Palm and Corn Salad

Serves: 12

Makes a perfect scooping salads, using fried (crisp) plantain chips as serving spoons. This salad is ever-present on many South Florida restaurant tables.

Ingredients:

16	oz.	Black beans, cooked
10	oz.	Corn, grilled
7	oz.	Heart of palm, quartered
2	each	Tomato, diced
1/2	each	Red onion, julienne
1/4	cup	Olive oil
3	tbs.	Lime juice, fresh
1/2	cup	Cilantro, chopped
2	heads	Lolla rosa baby lettuce
1	head	Red Belgium endive

Hints:

This salad brings out the best combination of Florida veggies accented with a Latino flair.

Instructions:

Mix the oil and lime juice. Toss the rest of the ingredients together with the dressing. Serve as close to service time as possible. Place on plate atop individual leaves of (red) Belgium endive and Lolla Rosa.

To make this salad truly "Southern", substitute black-eyed peas for the black beans.

Grilled Quail Salad with Jackfruit Salad

Serves: 2

Ingredients:

4	each	Quail, semi-boneless
1/4+1/4	cup	French vinaigrette, your own recipe
1	each	Portabello, grilled, sliced on the bias
1	cup	Baby (Mesclun) field greens
1	each	Jackfruit pod, julienned
1/2	teas.	Thicken up, food starch-found in health food stores
As needed		Pansies, or any other edible flower

Instructions:

Make the vinaigrette, mix half the jackfruit (with the first half of the French dressing-**your recipe**) with a handmixer. Add the thicken-up and let the blender run to thicken slightly. Toss in the other julienned jackfruit after finished with blending. Save until needed. Use the other half of the french dressing to marinate the bird.

To marinate and cook, just toss the quail into the dressing and make sure they are well coated. Place in refrigerator for 30 minutes, then heat, grill and cook them over grey coals. Grill the mushroom as well. Let cool. Slice on the bias later for a garnish, (see picture page 86). Place the greens in a bowl and toss with the reserved vinaigrette. Place in the center of the plate, with the birds slightly off to one side of each stack of greens. Garnish with chopped or whole flowers.

Jackfruit tastes of a
musky-flavored canteloupe.

Free-range quail can easily be found over the entire state. There is a special ranch in central Florida that offers an exceptional product. If there is someone in your family that is a hunter, you will find yourself using this recipe a lot.

Grilled Radicchio pockets with Crab

Serves: 4

Ingredients:

1 1/2	cups	Basmati rice, cooked, keep warm
1/2	cup	Bok choy, finely julienned
1	teas.	Garlic, crushed
1	tbs.	Shallots, finely chopped
2	tbs.	Bell pepper medley, brunoise
1	oz.	Olive oil, extra-virgin
As needed		Salt and pepper, 5:1 ratio
1/2	cup	Blue crab meat, pick over
16	each	Radicchio leaves, outer leaves, blanched
8	each	Chive spears
As needed		Cilantro, chopped
As needed		Red bell pepper, fine brunoise

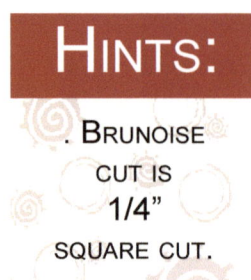

Hints:

. Brunoise cut is 1/4" square cut.

Instructions:

Sweat the shallots in the oil until they are transparent. Add the light green colored bok choy leaves. Cook until just limp. Add the crab, slowly heating and toss to mix well.

Remove heat and add the bell pepper medley and add to the warm rice. Mix well and divide mixture into 8 portions. Take the radicchio leaves and trim any browned parts off. Blanch a few seconds in boiling water and shock in an ice bath. Do the same with the chive spears. Lay out the radicchio leaves on a flat surface and fill with rice and rollup into eight packages. Roll again in a second leaf and secure with the chive.

Over a heated, oiled grill, warm these packages slightly so they retain their uniformity, but receive some smoky flavor from the grill.

Alternate use:

Use for height on plate with seafood entrees.

I use this recipe as building blocks when using spring roll (or large wonton) wrappers as the outer leaves instead of the radicchio. To use, fill the spring roll wrappers, seal, let rest a little while then deep fry until they are crisp. Cut in half after cooking. Place upright on a plate. Then top with fish fillets to give the plate presentation height.

The Zip

A playground for the salad Enthusiast~ Avoid damp, soggy greens by using these dressings sparingly, keeping in mind a little goes a long way.

Salad essentials...

Beyond Iceberg, the variety of lettuces available to you at this moment is only limited by your imagination in how to use them.

For those of us that don't have the time (or the availability) to choose our greens separately, many grocers have salad bins that you can choose what you want.

HERE IS AN EASY CONVERSION FOR YOU TO USE WHEN BUYING PRE-MADE BAGS OF GREENS. 10 OZ. BAG EQUALS 4 OR 5 CUPS OF GREENS. AND THIS EQUALS ABOUT 4-5 SERVINGS FOR DINNER.

Very popular, and found in most grocery stores nowadays, is a variety of mixed baby greens called Mesclun (meaning a mixture). This mixture changes as the seasonal availability fluctuates. It is truly a great combination of flavors, textures and colors. I will describe each leaf variety for you in this section so you can visualize how they taste before you make your salad. Later you can substitute leaf varieties of what you think should be in your salad.

Radicchio common salad ingredient because of it's peppery, slightly bitter taste, always tossed with other milder greens to drown out it's lusty flavor. I say instead of separating it from the rest of the greens, break up a couple heads and toss them with a few of the dressing recipes that follow: citrus-pear, mango or opal-basil.

Oakleaf, a mainstay in the Mesclun mixture. Oakleaf lettuces are both red and green, look similar to oak leaves but that is where the similarity stops. Textures are firm yet tender and have delicious flavors.

Ta Soi, is a lamb's leaf relative. Soft pliable texture similar to Bibb lettuce with the slight snappy taste of arugula.

Lolla Rosa, is a tender, slightly curly red tinged leaf lettuce.

Watercress, another Mesclun favorite, has roundish edible leaves with a slight tangy-peppery flavor. This green is great by itself with just a simple french vinaigrette.

Belgian Endive, both red and blond leaf "endives" have a bitter edge to their taste. This green is sturdy enough to be used as a serving tool (like a spoon) for: salsa, compote salads or small chopped salads.

Salad basics...

After you have an idea about what tastes come from the different combinations of greens, you will need to prepare them.

When you bring your greens home from the grocer, seal them in plastic so your refrigerator doesn't get the chance to pull out their internal moisture.

All greens and especially the ones with more sturdy leaves, such as spinach, arugula and watercress, should be dunked into several changes of fresh water until all sand and grit is gone. Lift out and lightly shake out the excess water from all the crevices. Dry well, because any extra moisture on the leaves will dilute your dressing. Excess water also speeds in leaf breaking down and will become mushy.

Also, avoid damp, soggy salads by only dressing them right before you are ready to serve.

Salad makings...

PREPARATION:

In general, leafy greens are delicate. Always treat with care. Everything you do to wash them, dry them and store them lessens their distinctive taste and in most cases, texture. In lieu of just eating them straight out of the bag, treat them with kid-gloves.

Arrange the greens in a manner that is ornate to the eye.

Salad arrangements...

A favorite way I like to arrange baby greens is to gather in a bundle like a bouquet in your hand. Using the larger leaves, gather the bottoms together as you work outward. Take a pre-hollowed 2 inch section of a cucumber and insert the bouquet of salad greens into it. Set it on the plate upright like a vase holding a bouquet of flowers. Garnish around the plate with baby pear-shaped tomatoes and dots of dressing. See the picture on page 65.

Salad temptations...

Edible Flowers

Edible flowers are a special treat for salad lovers. Their taste ranges from cedar to peppery. Not all flowers (or their parts) can be eaten. Use only the flowers that are especially marked for eating in your grocery store produce section. The flowers from the florist are usually sprayed with pesticides. Edible flowers are not only a specialized type of flower but, they are grown totally different. Here is a description of my favorite petal melanges...

Rose petals...delicate color and delicate sweet flavor.

Pansies...slightly spicy flavor. Sometimes violets taste sweet-spicy.

Geraniums...come in many colors with varying shades orange. Cedar flavored.

Marigolds...mild peppery flavor.

Dianthus...flat red, pink or white flowers with a sweet-spicy clove-like flavor and aroma.

Salad embellishments...

Micro-sprouts~broccoli, diakon, sunflower and alfalfa.

Thin julienne stripes of vegetables~jicama, fennel, red peppers or hearts of palm.

Chopped dried fruits (mango, papaya, pineapple).

Try any of these simple ideas in addition to the "greens" on your salad plate.

Crispy fried tortilla chips~corn or flour shells cut into strips and fried.

Snipped fresh herbs~tarragon, dill, chives are the most commonly used.

Finely grated and potent flavor busters~citrus zest, ginger, turnips, radish including daikon.

Individual preferences and styles:

> Use whichever leaf lettuce that your are comfortable with for recipes within this book. I formatted most of the dressing recipes for baby mesclun greens.

Salad accolades...

What good ever came out of eating salads?

Everyone that is on a diet eat salads right? Well, what many people might think as deprivation of your body is actually better for you. Salads are great sources of vitamins your body needs. Three of the key body builders that are factored into salads are...

Vitamin C....found in all citrus products, peppers, strawberries, tomatoes, broccoli, cantaloupe, cauliflower and kale.

Beta Carotene (an antioxidant that helps proliferate Vitamin A in your body) is found in carrots, sweet potatoes, peaches, cantaloupe, leafy greens, tomatoes, apricots, winter squashes and mangos.

Folic acid (a B Vitamin)...found in leafy greens, broccoli, asparagus, whole grains, dried beans, and citrus

Salad math...

In some recipes it will ask for a cup of this or that. Use this chart as your measuring stick.

Greens:	Wt. purchased:	Measurement:
Arugula	1 oz.	1 cup
Belgian Endive	4 oz.	20 leaves
Bibb	12 oz.	4 cups torn
Curly Endive	12 oz.	10 cups torn
Escarole	8 oz.	7 cups torn
Iceberg	1 1/4 lbs.	10 cups torn
Leaf lettuce	12 oz.	8 cups torn
Radicchio	8 oz.	5 cups torn
Romaine	1 lb.	6 cups torn
Spinach	1 lb.	12 cups torn
Watercress	4 oz.	2 cups, without stems

ACHIOTE VINAIGRETTE

SERVES: 8-10

This vinaigrette makes a great marinade for chicken breast. When you remove the breast from this recipe, leave a little on the breast and saute it rapidly in a super hot pan. The marinade's color (after cooking) makes the final product look great.

INGREDIENTS:

8	oz.	Olive oil
2	oz.	Achiote seeds
1 1/2	oz.	Orange blossom honey
To taste		Cilantro
As needed		Salt and pepper
3	oz.	Cider vinegar
As needed		Emulsifier, "Pro-thick"-*SEE NOTE BELOW*
1/4	teas.	Vanilla, the real stuff-see recipe later in book

INSTRUCTIONS:

Soak seeds in oil 30 minutes. Bring to simmer, cook seeds 3 minutes. Strain. With the machine running, place the next four ingredients in food processor one at a time. Add this flavored oil last, slowly pouring it in to a make vinaigrette. Pour into a bowl, lightly sprinkle this emulsifier over the dressing and with a wire whip, stir in by hand. Thicken to the point where the whip wires leaves trials when drawn thorough the sauce.

"Prothick" is a commercial precooked granular food thickening starch. You can find a subsitute~Xanthan gum in health food stores.

Citrus-Pear vinaigrette

Serves: 8

Pear meaning Asian pear. This is one of my favorites. I usually garnish the finished product with the flowering buds of the herb - tarragon. The tarragon bud has a unique liquorice flavor that makes the taste combination one to remember.

Ingredients:

1/2	cup	Sherry vinegar
1	each	Grapefruit, juice
1	each	Orange, juice
1 1/2	oz.	Soy sauce
1	tbs.	Pickled ginger, finely chopped
1/2	tbs.	Ginger, finely crushed
1	tbs.	Chili puree
1/2	tbs.	Celery seeds
1 1/3	cups	Olive oil
4	oz.	Asian pear, cleaned, chopped
As needed		Salt and pepper, 5:1 ratio
1	tbs.	Citrus zest: grapefruit, orange, lime or lemon

Hints:

Besides using this recipe for salads, it has other uses, such as a garnishing-sauce on chicken and seafood plates.

Instructions:

Wash the citrus and then zest. Remove the sections of the fruit, save for garnishing, squeeze the pith's juices out after sectioning. Place the juices with the sherry vinegar and the next five ingredients in a Cuisinart. Mix well, adding the oil slowly. Add the pears and process until smooth. Season.

To Use:

When you are dressing a salad, use the orange sections as an added garnish for the salad. They can also be used as a garnish if you want to use the dressing on a chicken breast entree.

Ginger-Citrus Vinaigrette

Serves: 3

Uglifruit has the qualities of both Mandarine orange and grapefruit. They are named "ugli" fruit because of their loose fitting skin. They are grown in the Caribbean, and easily found in the winter at specialty grocers.

Ingredients:

2	TBS.	Lime juice
6	TBS.	Uglifruit juice
2	TBS.	Rice wine vinegar
1	TBS.	Scallions, chopped
2	TEAS.	Ginger, fresh, chopped
1/2	TEAS.	Garlic, finely chopped
1	TBS.	Soy sauce
1	TBS.	Sesame oil
5	TBS.	Canola oil
As needed		Salt & pepper, 5:1 ratio

Hints: Use as a marinade for grilled shrimp. Marinate 30 minutes and use as a mop to brush on as you grill.

Instructions:
Reduce juices over heat until only two tablespoons remain. Let cool. Whisk in the next five ingredients. Add the oils and emulsifying in a high speed blender. Season.

Mango Mayo

Serves: 30

Ingredients:

1	QT.	Mayo
1	EACH	Mango, soft, over-ripe
2	TBS.	Honey
1	EACH	Scotch Bonnet pepper, fine
1	TBS.	Salt
7	EACH	Cornichon (a small French pickle)

Hints: This recipe is a natural with conch fritters.

Instructions:
Pulse/mix all (except pickle) in a cuisinart. Cut the pickle by hand and fold into sauce for visual effect. This recipe keeps well in the refrigerator for weeks.

Spicy Mango-Seville coulis

Serves: 4

A coulis is a puree of ingredients enhanced with juice and vinegar. This combination of sweet and sour is the perfect example of how to form recipes with a "Yin and Yang" balance.

Ingredients:

1	cup	Mango pulp, chopped
1/4	cup	Sugar
4	each	Garlic, crushed
1/2	each	Scotch bonnet pepper
4	tbs.	Vinegar, brown rice wine
1/3	cup	Seville orange (sour orange) juice
1/4	teas.	Cumin seeds, dry toasted in a skillet

Instructions:

Grind pulp in food processor and strain. Mix the pulp with the sugar and heat in a heavy-bottomed pot until thickened. Remove from heat, cool. Grind toasted cumin seeds in coffee grinder. In food processor, add the thickened puree, garlic and the next three ingredients. Blend well. Season.

Opal-Basil vinaigrette

Serves: 10

This makes a great marinade when grilling. Marinate chicken breast for three hours.

Ingredients:

1	cup	Raspberry vinegar
1/4	cup	Shallots, diced
3	cup	Olive oil
1	tbs.	Orange juice, concentrate
3	bunch	Opal-basil, chopped
1	teas.	Honey, an orange blossom variety
As needed		Salt and pepper
1	each	Egg yolk
10	drops	Tabasco

Instructions:

Blend the first two ingredients in a cuisinart. Add the oil slowly and then the concentrate. Add the leaves and the seasoning and flavorings. Add the yolk and mix well. Then add the tabasco as needed to your tastes.

Passionfruit-Chipotle Vinaigrette

Serves: 8

This is a perfect glaze for roasted Porkloin. Brush with the vinaigrette while it is cooking in the oven.

Ingredients:

2	tbs.	Garlic kernels, fine chopped
4	tbs.	Shallots, finely chopped
1	qt.	Passionfruit juice
1	cup	Cider vinegar
2	tbs.	Orange juice concentrate
1	tbs.	Dry chipotle peppers, ground fine
3	tbs.	Salt, kosher
2	oz.	Corn syrup
1	tbs.	Vanilla extract, see recipe page
1	cup	Olive oil, extra-virgin
1	teas.	Prothick, food starch

Hints: Sweet, sassy and packs a wallop. The taste of Passionfruit is beyond description. It's taste encompasses the essence of Guava with a citrus taste-bud punch.

Instructions:

Mix the first 5 ingredients and reduce over high heat until reduced to 3/4 cup. Add the next 4 ingredients and cool. Strain. Slowly mix in the oil with a immersion blender. Then add the thickener. Let it run while slowly sprinkling in the thickener. Run for 5 minutes. The sauce should thickened, enough so the dressing will adhere to what it is added to.

Uglifruit "Coulis-grette"

Serves: 10

Use for seafood, fish fillets or poultry.

Ingredients:

10	each	Uglifruit, juice and zest
1/3	cup	Shallots, chopped
1	each	Bay leaf
3	each	Thyme branches
1/2	cup	Sake
2	oz.	Rice wine vinegar
8	oz.	Olive oil, extra-virgin
As needed		Salt
To taste		Tabasco sauce
2	oz.	Cane sugar syrup
1	tbs.	Prothick-food starch
		Con't on next page

INSTRUCTIONS:
REDUCE THE FIRST 5 INGREDIENTS OVER HIGH HEAT UNTIL REDUCED TO ABOUT 3/4 CUP. STRAIN, COOL, PLACE IN A CUISINART AND ADD THE VINEGAR. FLAVOR WITH TOBASCO, SALT AND CANE SYRUP. THEN SLOWLY ADD THE OIL. WITH THE MACHINE RUNNING, ADD THE PROTHICK AND LET RUN FOR THREE MINUTES. BLEND UNTIL A SALAD DRESSING CONSISTENCY IS ATTAINED. CHECK SEASONING AND FLAVOR.

TO USE:
USE AS A DRESSING FOR GRILLED CHICKEN SALADS OR AS A GLAZE ON POULTRY OR MOST ANY STRONG FLAVORED FISH LIKE; WAHOO BY GLAZING AFTER THEY ARE GRILLED. OR PLACE ON THE PLATE BEFORE SETTING INTO PLACE.

HINTS:
UGLIFRUIT...IS A JAMAICAN FRUIT WITH LOOSE FITTING, MIS-FORMED SKIN~HENCE THE NAME. DOES NOT HAVE A LOT OF SEEDS AND HAS A SWEET-PUNGENT TASTE. THIS FRUIT WAS DEVELOPED BY CROSSING A GRAPEFRUIT AND MANDARIN ORANGE (TANGERINE). AVAILABLE IN THE WINTER AND SPRING FROM JANUARY TO MAY.

CURRIED MANGO YOGURT DRESSING
SERVES: 10
THIS CAN BE USED FOR A COLD POTATO SALAD DRESSING OR AS A DIP FOR AN APPETIZER.

INGREDIENTS:

1/2	PINT	NON-FAT YOGURT
1/4	CUP	CURRY POWER
1/3	TEAS.	CELERY SEEDS
1	EACH	LIME, JUICED
1/4	CUP	MANGO CHUTNEY
1	TBS.	GINGER
2	TBS.	SHALLOTS
1	TBS.	GARLIC
6	SPRIGS	CILANTRO
3	SPRIGS	MINT
1-2	TEAS.	PROTHICK, THICKENING AGENT

INSTRUCTIONS:
USING A HAND MIXER, MIX ONE INGREDIENT AT A TIME INTO THE YOGURT. ADD THE THICKENER LAST. CHILL.

HINTS:
THIS WILL MAKE A GREAT DRESSING FOR A LOW-FAT CHICKEN SALAD, REPLACING MAYO.

LE REPERTOIRE

IMAGINATION............
                      .
                      .
                      .
                      . IS THE NEXT STEP
                ABOVE .
                      .
                      .
                      .
                      .
                      .
                      .
                      .

KNOWLEDGE.

Duplicating foodways....

Imagine if you will, crystal clear, aqua blue waters merging with an equally blue sea at the horizon. The surf is roaring while palm trees are swaying towards the condo-lined beach front.

Scanning down the steamy asphalt, Europeans transverse the boulevard that separates the sands of South Beach from the refurbished "Deco" hotels. Wisps of French, German and Spanish are heard over the squawking of parrots of what a wonderful time everyone had in the "Magic-City".

It is the nocturnal social life that attracts most to the Art Deco District-SoBe. Within the pages of this book I will try to duplicate for you the experience of witnessing the birth of a new cuisine. As the chef, you ponder all these circumstances in your "Kingdom du Jour" - you realize that this spectacle isn't a fantasy. You are in the New American Riviera, once deemed the HOTTEST place in the nation for new culinary awakenings.

When a chef aspires to duplicate Florida's Fusion Cuisine, he must be able to mingle the ideologies and the methodologies of our local residents. That is: native inhabitants, old southerners (people from the deep southern states), Asians who were brought to the outlying islands to replace the African freed slaves, the Caribbean melange of cultures and the influences of various Latin American cultures.

Many times there is a plating theme. There are sometimes five individual recipes mingling on the plate including; starches, vegetables, a protein and multiple sauces to every new plate presentation. Plates can also be stylized in a way that depicts an individual cooking heritage. One item on the plate might be prepared in the style of the West Indies, another item might be cooked in a classical southern tradition and, another might be cooked as Florida's earliest settlers (native Americans) might have.

Conversations with a local farmer inform you that a crop of Atemoya is available. A whirlwind of ideas comes brimming up as you start to ponder the various uses for this product. You think that it might be used as a coulisgrette, sorbet, creme brulee, ice cream, beurre blanc, marinade, sorbet, fruit cup, salad dressing or a sauce reduction for seafood, poultry or pork. You decide to marinate the fresh quails that you just received this morning, in a curry rub and then quickly grill the birds over north Florida oak and finally blast them with a "coulisgrette" of the atemoya.

The New American Riviera is the only place in this Nation that has enough energy to fuel this cuisine-machine. The Chef has to be able to transmute the energies of SoBe to his canvas...the plate. With some locally procured Tropical ingredients and some imagination, this style can be reproduced by all of us.

Deco

Your travel agent called it the "Art Deco District", but to locals it is SoBe (South Beach). At every turn in the Art Deco District, renovated deco-period hotels sporting intimate cafes and plush dining rooms have become commonplace. As you stop and shop at world-reknown designer shops, you notice that the fashions on the streets resemble something that could be worn in any fashion capital around the world. As in fashion, new culinary concepts will always be the in thing to do. The birthplace of the latest new culinary trend is the same place where the Old World found the New...

AS ONE WALKS THE STREETS OF DECO, YOU CAN SEE MANY THINGS……

In Deco, models, model-wannabes, model-chasers and model-makers are all found at these "in" places. Commercials, publicity shoots, movies, and television series are being produced here. The New American Riviera is bringing the famous and the struggling to our shores. As retro fashions become the rage once again, so do the previous food trends.

IN FOODS, AS WELL AS IN FASHIONS, ANYTHING GOES IN THE DECO DISTRICT.

The local Art Deco District is abuzz with new construction. Miami, once said to be the "Capital of South America", is truly a gateway to America for many South American investors. Nowadays, it is a great investment for foreign tycoons to renovate a historic building and squeeze in a plushly decorated intimate dining room. These hotels continue to bring chic jet setters from around the world to Miami Beach. Fusion chefs have meld these world traveler's amiable tastes into new menu selections. Many restaurants in the early nineteen-ninety's were cooking as your mother did. They were developing an "Americana" style of menu format. Americana usually meant meatloaf and mashed potatoes, but in South Florida they would get a special twist. Here the chef will use turkey instead of beef in a meatloaf and will serve it with a "jus" thickened by natural reduction. The potatoes will probably have an addition of locally available boniato or malanga to give it a new taste variance.

In the Deco District, chefs have to lighten foods the way mom never thought about to keep them fashionably heart healthy. The rest of the country's fascination in keeping foods lighter in fats and salt has led our chefs to develop notable plates that highlight these methods. They use intensive flavor reductions to boost the taste of an entree. They realize that if the food doesn't have a distinctively specialized taste, its presentation is of minimal importance.

Of course no one broils anymore. Chefs use wood grills to cook meats, fish, and veggies. They substitute local varieties of seafood for once classic Americana northern fish species. New England has a good many varieties of seafood, but nothing compared to Florida.

Even the modern "French Nouvelle" classics have to be revised. Beurre blancs, a standard of any French Nouvelle plate, is updated by using local products like: lichee, mango, citrus, loquat, or atemoya as a base flavor. What is making this new regional cuisine so popular is its new exotic allure. Previously unheard of tropical foods are becoming commonplace in this new regional cuisine.

Just as Columbus and Ponce de Leon came to these shores searching for the new and unexperienced, so do the food junkies in this new century. As the bohemian styles of the 1960's changed American eating habits forever, so will Florida's Fusion Foods after the year 2010. Products from the "New World" are once again establishing themselves on dinner menus around this country and abroad.

FLAVOR

BBQ cure....for Duck Breast

Serves: 10

Ingredients:

3	each	Coladas, see the FYI chapter, page 17
2	oz.	Dark Soy sauce
As needed		Guarapo, pressed juice from sugarcane
2	tbs.	Kahlua Liquor

Instructions:
Mix all ingredients. Set a Moulade (or Muscovy) duck breast into marinade overnight to cure. Grill breast the next day over hot coals until just pink inside. Grill on a rack about 5 inches from the heat of the coals.

Hint...Cook Muscovy duck breast about 12 minutes on the skin side, flip and cook five minutes on the other side. Let rest and cool slightly before slicing so the juices have a chance to flow back out towards the edges of the breast. Serve with a mango salsa and a natural grain rice.

B.B.Q. Meat Rub

Serves: 10

A true "Old Southern" standard in the kitchen.

Ingredients:

2	tbs.	Salt
2	tbs.	Sugar
2	tbs.	Brown sugar
2	tbs.	Chili powder
2	tbs.	Black pepper
1	tbs.	Cayenne pepper
2	tbs.	Cumin seeds, toasted in skillet,

Instructions:
Mix all dry ingredients well in a coffee grinder. Rub into meat before smoking or grilling. Cook as instructed per recipe.

Hints: This recipe should make enough for a couple Pork butts or 12 slabs of ribs.

Chili-cocoa dust

Serves: 15 - decorated plates

Hints:

A taste bud blaster.

Ingredients:
10	each	Ancho chilies, dry
2	tbs.	Cocoa powder
2	tbs	Kosher salt
1	tbs.	Garlic, granular
1	tbs.	Brown sugar

Instructions:
Bake the chilies until brown and dry. Cool. Crush in a Cuisinart. Add the rest of the ingredients and puree fine. Store in covered jar.

Use to dust the rim of plates or make decorative designs on food, etc. Use on the rim of a "chili" cup so someone can sip from its side and get a real taste sensation.

Chimichurri

Serves: 12

Hints:

A variable multi purpose tool. Refreshing and memorable.

Ingredients:
2	bunches	Parsley
4	each	Garlic, crushed
1/2	cup	Olive oil
1/3	cup	Lime juice
1/4	cup	Cream sherry
1/2	teas.	White pepper
1/2	teas.	Salt

Instructions:
Mix all in a food processor. Make sure it is pureed fine. Store in covered jar. Keep in refrigerator.

This also can be used as a crust or marinade for all sorts of seafood and served with churrasco steak. You can add *scotch bonnet chilies* to intensify the heat, do so carefully!

Herbena-Chimichurri
Serves: 12

Ingredients:

4	bunches	Lemon herbena
4	each	Garlic, crushed
1/2	cup	Olive oil
1/3	cup	Lime juice
1/4	cup	Cream sherry
1/2	teas.	White pepper
1/2	teas.	Salt
2	oz.	Sugarcane juice

Hints: Use as a seasoning compound for seafood and chicken breast

Instructions:
Mix all in food processor, adding cane juice as the mixer is churning. Make sure it is pureed finely. Store in covered jar. Keep in refrigerator.

Seafood "Creole" seasons
Serves: 10

Ingredients:

1	tbs.	Oregano, dry
1	teas.	Salt
2	tbs.	Garlic, granulated
1	teas.	Black pepper
1/3	teas.	Cayenne pepper
1	tbs.	Thyme, dry
2	tbs.	Paprika

Instructions:
Mix all in a Cuisinart. Sprinkle over foods before baking or grilling. Use one of the marinades from this book as the "glue" to hold these seasonings in place on the food before they are placed in the oven.

To Use:
Use any of the marinades in this book; like papaya, passionfruit or citrus for an extra zing. Then dip marinated seafood lightly into the seasoning and then place into a pan to sear.

Onion Crust

Serves: 12

Use for topping on a variety of fish or as a coating for potato planks.

Ingredients:

1	recipe	Southwestern crust, see recipe on page 85
2	cup	Red onions, sliced, deep fried brown
1	tbs.	Onion seeds, toasted and ground

Instructions:

Make the southwestern crust. Deep fry the onions until they brown completely. Dry on paper towels. Quickly toast the seeds in a super hot wok for 2 minutes. Add both to the crust when cooled. Mix in the food processor.

**** A variation of this recipe is also great, add 7 tbs. (of the **dry** ingredient package) of Thai peanut sauce mix to the crust after mixing the rest of this recipe. - This can be found in most Asian markets.

Salmon or Wahoo Marinade

Serves: 10

Ingredients:

1/2	cup	Orange juice concentrate
2	oz.	Triple sec liquor
2	tbs.	Orange zest
2	tbs.	Key lime juice
1	tbs.	Black pepper
3	tbs.	Juniper berries, crushed
2	tbs.	Kosher salt
6	tbs.	Sugar

Instructions:

Mix all ingredients and heat to a simmer to release their flavors. Cool.

To use....

Marinate salmon (or other rich tasting fillets of fish like wahoo) for three hours before cooking. Brush over the fillets as they cook over white hot coals.

Southwestern Crust

Serves: 12

Can be used for crusted potatoes that have been dipped into melted butter first and baked in an oven.

Ingredients:

2/3	cup	Yellow cornmeal
1/3	cup	Toasted bread crumbs
1/4	cup	Parmesan cheese
1	tbs.+1 teas	Chili powder
1	tbs.+1 teas	Cumin, ground
1	tbs.+1 teas	Garlic powder
1	teas.	Sugar
1	teas	Cayenne red pepper

Hints: For use with seabass, grouper or snapper fillets.

Instructions:

Grind all spices and seasonings together in a coffee grinder. Mix the dry spices with the bread crumbs and cornmeal. Remove from grinder, in a separate bowl toss in the cheese.

Seafood Spice Rub

Serves: 20

Ingredients:

2	teas.	Allspice
2	teas.	Brown sugar
2	teas.	Sugar
2	teas.	Cayenne pepper
1	teas.	Salt
1	teas.	Black pepper
1	teas.	Chives (dry)
1	teas.	Basil (dry)
1	teas.	Ginger, ground
1	teas.	Paprika
1	teas.	Thyme (dry)
1	teas.	Garlic powder

Hints: If you are looking for something special for swordfish filets, try this recipe.

Instructions:

Grind all into dust in coffee grinder. Do in small batches to insure even grinding. Store in jar for up to 6 months. Use to top any fish fillet before baking, broiling or grilling.

SEABASS WITH SOUTHWESTERN CRUST, FROM PREVIOUS PAGE
BERRY RICE, SEE PAGE 181 AND SIMPLE PASSIONFRUIT SAUCE,
SEE PAGE 108 WITH PAPAYA GARNI.

WILD POULTRY RUBBED
QUAIL SALAD PAGE 88.
WITH A HOMESTEAD
CORN COMPOTE, SEE
PAGE 168

BIGEYE TUNA WITH YIN AND YANG MARINADE, SEE PAGE 89
PINEAPPLE CARPACCIO AND ORANGE-MAPLE-ALLSPICE GLAZE
ON PAGE 106-107

GULF BLACK GROUPER, CHILI-COCOA DUST, SEE PAGE 82
FIG PUREE, SEE PAGE 156, CALAMONDIN SAUCE, SEE PAGE 99

Sofrito

Serves: 12

Ingredients:
2	oz.	Salt pork, diced
2	tab.	Lard with annatto
1	ea.	Onion, chopped
1	ea.	Garlic, fine
1	ea.	Green bell pepper, finly chopped
6	oz.	Tomato, concasse
As needed		Salt and pepper, 5:1 ratio

Instructions:
Saute salt pork with seasoned lard to release fat. Cook slowly up to 20 minutes. Saute veggies. Add tomato concasse. Simmer 15 minutes, season and cool. Jar and refrigerate.

You may grind this recipe in a Cuisinart and use it as a rub for pork, or a flavoring ingredient for sauces, soups, stews, etc.

Hints:
For use atop poultry when roasting. Not a "Spa" style recipe.

Wild Poultry rub

Serves: 10

Ingredients:
2	teas.	Sea salt
1	teas.	Black pepper
1/2	teas.	Thyme, dry
1/2	teas.	Sage, dry

Instructions:
Grind in a coffee grinder until all are smooth.

To Use:
Just dust marinated poultry with the spices. The marinade helps keep the spice clinging to the birds as they roast.

Hints:
Use for duck breast, chicken, quail and pork dishes. Great when combined with an Asian sauce or one with sweeter overtones.

Yin and Yang marinade

Serves: 10

Ingredients:

6	oz.	Tamari (light)
1	bunch	Cilantro, chopped
4	tbs.	Ginger, fine
4	tbs.	Garlic, fine
1/2	cup	Sesame oil
3	each	Limes, juiced and zest
To taste		Chili puree, with garlic

Instructions:
Mix all.

To Use: spread over the chicken. Let marinate for at least 3 hours. Grill breast and finish cooking in an oven until done. Cool, slice to order for salads or platter.

Hints: For use only in small batches. Separate and jar. Keeps indefinitely.

Yucatan Spice rub

Serves: 25

I have added this recipe because when it is used on pork, it will turn you into a "the other white meat" lover.

Ingredients:

12	each	Garlic kernals, whole in skin
2	teas.	Oregano
1	teas.	Black peppercorns, ground
1/4	teas.	Allspice berries, ground
1/4	teas.	Cumin seeds, ground
1/2	teas.	Salt
1	tbs..	Cider vinegar
2	tbs.	Seville orange

Instructions:
Roast garlic and then mash with the back of a knife. Cool. Grind all spices and herbs. Add the mashed garlic. Add the vinegar and juice. Mix into thick paste. Store in a covered jar. Refrigerate until needed.

To use:
Liberally spread across a roast before cooking.

Hints: Use for; rubbing onto meats (especially pork or game) or, used as a finishing condiment for sauces, soup and stews. Use it also as is flavoring oils for salads.

Taste... Paradigms in Flavor

TASTE, a scientific look.

Tropical cookery is the new... PARADIGM in FLAVOR!

The most significant food trend in this past decade is FLAVOR. Our local menus feature exotic tropical flavors that are characteristically complex.

These exotic flavors are paired on the plate in such a way to tell a story. One that tells of our cookery heritage, cultural preference and food interrelationships. A South Florida chef will develop new combinations of flavors that recites the heart and soul of a South Florida culinary attitude. Our locally-grown tropical provisions make it possible for more creativity, unusual combinations and a surprising blend of flavor.

In doing this a South Florida chef pairs the exotic and lesser recognized local food rarities with something well known, to create a soul-satisfying "Taste-Variance".

TASTE-VARIANCE ?
What is it?
It is why you are buying a new cookbook.

The purchase of a new cookbook doesn't guarantee that your feast is going to be a culinary masterpiece. It only helps in its formation.

People that buy new cookbooks yearn for new tastes. Differing your usual dinner tastes is what most people want when experimenting with a new cookbook. Developing a new repertoire, one should try to balance the entire plate's taste. This is where the macrobiotic idea of Yin and Yang is addressed. It is the counterbalancing of flavors...spicy and sweet, sweet and tangy....that gives your tastebuds enjoyment. I have tried to incorporate basic Yin and Yang Taste-Variances in all the recipes within your new cookbook.

What we are trying to do throughout this book is to build a sensory eruption. To be proficient at this mission you will have to understand the basics of a taste-variance. An overview of the basics of taste perceptions are...

- Flavor–is built by the cook and is realized by the senses. Your palate and your nose work as a sense-o-gram. It meters and tells your brain the chemical reaction factors.
- Thermal (hot, cold)–trigeminal (signal brain to notice) and Umami (fullness of the tastes) feelings are all part of the tasting process.
- Textures–is it crunchy, soft or liquidy? Foods are paired to combine these factors on a plate to stimulate other senses while eating.
- Kinesthetic–(feel)–how does it coat your palate?
- Auditory–sounds involved while chewing?
- Temporal effects–how and why does this food affect your eating and your conscious enjoyment.
- Order of Occurrence–how are the taste, textures and fullness of flavors organized on a plate.
- Impact–what is the flavor impact of this dish? Does the sauce jump out at your tastebuds?
- Training, anchoring to references–what mom used to cook. Or what culinary schools do well, they get young chefs in training, eating something that they might not have had before. Giving them the correct education on how these foods are properly prepared and the knowledge to adapt (or relate) this education to the inexperienced so they can prepare new food items intelligently.
- Duration–how long does the aroma or kick of the recipe linger?
- Carry through–do flavors linger and impart a deep taste that stirs all the tasting senses?
- Aromatics–as one might think, aromatics have to be translated by the nose. The more aromatic a herb or essence might be, the easier it is for the nose to recognize it. Strictly a temporal affect, the aroma of foods are the first or second sense used while eating. While you are eating, the aromas are rising up to your nose as the food enters your mouth and, they are drawn up in a back-flow method from the back of your throat as you are chewing.
- Fats–(in most cases we are speaking of animal fats) The development of flavor is often caused by the amount of, and how fats are used in a recipe. The role of fats are to be a source of the flavor and they will help your senses realize flavor.

    They supply and enhance temporal effects of the subunits (starch, veggie, sauce, etc....) on the plate. They act as a precursor to flavor. They also mask foods if used in the wrong proportions. Most importantly, they impart (in every food) a feeling noticed by the palate of richness, coating the palate with a layer of fat telling your senses that this food is rich. To most people, the sensation of richness in foods in an important one. Fats release flavor to the senses in different ways varying on how much fat is used in a preparation.

Flavor, intensity and time are inversely related when fats are used in a recipe. As time progresses (after the food is eaten) flavors diminish. High fat concentrations in foods will increase their length of time that the flavor is experienced. This means fatty foods are felt (tasted) longer. Fat-free foods give a short intense burst of flavor.

How are we trained to realize flavors.

The origins of our feelings about foods are based in our earliest childhood training. The attitudes of these feelings are structured by several occurrences...
- Biological-myself, I can't eat foods made with Accent (MSG) because of the head aches that follow afterwards.
- Psychological-you just can't get by the fact that escargot are still snails.
- Social Customs-being of the Kosher faction limits your occurrences of tasting pork and related food items.
- Opportunity-how many Americans have the opportunity to taste the difference between a northern Italian truffle and a truffle from France.
- Private associations-to me, snails are snails no matter the name.
- Pleasure-sweets are something that I can't give up because of the intense palate pleasure when eaten.
- Pain-astringent foods are my downfall. An under-ripe Persimmon (or the Asian - Bitter melon) is something that my tastebuds can't stand.

These occurrence are formulated by memories from childhood to adulthood.
These tasting responses are learned by....
- Anecdotal-when you can remember from your childhood the inferences about chopped liver, resembling baby food (or its after product).
- Literature-you can assimilate what a food tastes like by matching it's description of flavor by foods you are already cognitive of.

Simply Tasting-eat, eat, eat...
Exposure to the world of food-experience all that is new. You will never know what that prehistoric looking Rollinia tastes like if you never give it a try.
Cooking-get involved and experiment. Trial and error forms a new cuisine. Developing a new cuisine is as easy as pairing something known with an unknown.

Sauces...

"Taste Enhancers"
Always bring out the "Spite" in each presentation.

Walloping your tastebuds with a handful of flavor

Apricot-Ginger Glaze

Serves: 8

This sauce is great for grilled porkloin, and a glaze for shellacing salmon, tuna, shrimp, scallops or chicken breast.

Ingredients:

6	oz.	Mirin
2	inch	Ginger piece
4	oz.	Apricot jam
2	teas.	Satay sauce (dry), found in an Asian market
As needed		Salt and pepper
1	teas.	Tamari
1	oz.	Ponzu
4	oz.	Chicken stock

Instructions:

Simmer the mirin and the ginger for about four minutes in a stainless steel pot, so the flavors of the ginger leach out. Add the apricot jam and let melt into the sauce mix. Add the satay sauce and let cook about three more minutes. Add the rest of the ingredients and taste for a slight hint of acidity. Season. Strain. Cool.

Anaheim-Vanilla Syrup

Serves: 10

Ingredients:

3	cups	Mandarin juice, reduced to 1 cup.
2	teas.	Triple sec
3	tbs.	Corn syrup
1	oz.	Chablis
1	teas.	Homemade vanilla, see recipe page 112
1	each	Anaheim chilies, rough chopped
1	teas.	Cider vinegar

Hints: Use for chili topping or glazing of poultry. Can be used as a base for "coulisgrettes".

Instructions:

Reduce the juice over a high flame until 1 cup of liquid is achieved. Add triple sec and next two ingredients. Reduce again by half. Add the rest of the ingredients and cook down until a syrupy glaze is acquired.

Grilled white tuna (escolar) with seafood spice page 85
and apricot-ginger glaze, page 95
Anaheim-vanilla syrup, page 95 and nectarines.

Wood-grilled, Uglifruit "coulis-grette", see page 74-75 marinated shrimp (on sugarcane skewer) and tuna with a red curry, grapefruit and guava sauce, page 101

Guava B.B.Q. basting sauce, see page 103 Wood-grilled wahoo. micro-greens garnish. Set on top a BogBerry sweet potato Terrine, see page 176

South Florida style Apple Cider sauce

Serves: 8

You might not think apples should go into a South Florida cookbook, but in the upper regions of north Florida apples do grow. It happens that these apples, usually smaller make for a slightly astringent juice, so I have added guarapo to smooth out the tastes.

Ingredients:

1	qt.	Apple cider
3/4	cup	Rice wine vinegar
1/2	cup	Chardonnay wine
1/4	cup	Shallots, finely chopped
1/2	each	Vanilla beans, split
1	each	Scotch bonnets, chopped
1	each	Anaheim peppers, chopped
2	cups	Guarapo, see note on page 17
1	inch	Ginger, crushed/chopped fine
6	inch	Lemongrass, chop finely

Hints:

This is a very potent glaze. I use it for chicken breast, pork loin, pork tenderloin, etc..... Brush over meats as they cook on the grill.

Instructions:

Cook the first four ingredients. Then add the vanilla and the peppers. Let everything boil rapidly until the volume of liquid is reduced to 2/3 of the original amount. Mix the sauce with a hand held mixer to puree all the contents. Add the rest of the ingredients and let simmer for 30 minutes. Strain. Save until needed.

This recipe includes all five culinary represented flags my fusion cookery. These ingredients represent southern America, Native, Oriental, Islands and Latin American cookery. The clear taste and amber appearance of the cider goes a long way in punctuating this recipe.

Calamondin sauce

Serves: 10

Use with grilled chicken breast or seafood.

Ingredients:

1/2	gal	Calamondin fruits, peeled
1/3	cup	Shallots, finely diced
4	each	Bay leaf
1/3	cup	Apple cider vinegar
1	qt.	Chardonnay wine
1	qt.	Chicken demi-glace, reduced
1	lb.	Butter, softened
As needed		Flour
As needed		Honey
As needed		Salt & pepper, 5:1 ratio

Instructions:

Reduce the first five ingredients over high heat until reduced to a light glaze (the consistency of honey). Add the demi-glace and reduce again by half. Toss chunks of butter into flour and then add the flour dusted butter to the sauce whipping them in slowly. Let simmer and thicken slightly. Season and flavor to your taste.

Hints:

Calamondin looks like and is treated as a tiny sweet and sour orange. This sauce will explode on your palate with the taste of intensely tart citrus. It could be used as a shellac on various poultry dishes and works extremely well accompanying roasted Long Island duck.

Cilantro aioli

Serves: 10-15

After the sauce is cool, funnel into a squeeze bottle. Use as a garnishing sauce for plates and individual appetizers. Use to garnish the crab sandwich on page 51.

Ingredients:

1	bunch	Cilantro, leaves only
1/2	teas.	Salt
1	teas.	Garlic, chopped
1	dash.	Pernod
1/2	teas.	Lime juice
1/4	cup	Olive oil
5	drops	Tabasco
1 1/2	oz.	Cooked boiled potatoes, skinless, chopped

Con't on next page.....

Hints:

This sauce will thicken by itself after refrigeration.

INSTRUCTIONS:
GRIND FIRST FIVE INGREDIENTS IN THE CUISINEART UNTIL WELL PUREED. ADD THE OIL IN SLOWLY TO FORM AN EMULSIFICATION. DROP IN THE CHUNKS OF COOKED POTATO AS THE MACHINE, AND LET RUN UNTIL YOU CAN'T SEE ANY CHUNKS OF THE POTATO IN THE MIXTURE. STRAIN/PUSH THROUGH A CHINOISE STRAINER. REFRIGERATE

CHERIMOYA BEURRE BLANC

SERVES: 8-10

INGREDIENTS:

1	EACH	BAY LEAF, BRUISED
4	OZ.	SHALLOT, FINE
1	CUP	APPLE CIDER VINEGAR
3/4	QT.	WHITE WINE
2	OZ.	RUM, DARK
6	(1/2 #)	CHERIMOYA, CLEANED, DE-SEEDED
3/4	QT.	HEAVY CREAM
1	TEAS.	VANILLA
3/4	LB.	BEURRE MANIE (CHUNKS, WHOLE BUTTER TOSSED IN FLOUR)
2	TBS.	SUGAR
1/2	TBS.	SALT AND PEPPER, 5:1 RATIO

HINTS:

CHERIMOYA IS THE WORLD'S BEST TASTING FRUIT.

USE A STAINLESS STEEL POT FOR THE REDUCTION.

INSTRUCTIONS:
REDUCE THE FIRST SIX INGREDIENTS OVER HIGH HEAT TO HALF OF THE ORIGINAL VOLUME. WHIP TO BREAK UP FRUIT. ADD THE CREAM AND REDUCE AGAIN BY HALF. FLAVOR, TASTE AND CORRECT SEASONINGS. MONTAGE AU BEURRE (WHIP IN FLOUR COATED, CHUNKS OF WHOLE BUTTER). KEEP SAUCE JUST WARM UNTIL READY TO SERVE. IF THE SAUCE GETS TO HOT, THE BUTTER WILL BREAK OUT OF SOLUTION AND FLOAT UP AND SIT ON TOP THE SAUCE MAKING AN UNSIGHTLY MESS ON THE PLATE.

THIS RECIPE CAN BE USED WITH EQUAL WEIGHTS OF ANY
EXOTIC FRUIT WITH A LITTLE SEASONING ADJUSTMENTS.
THIS IS NOT A "SPA" STYLE RECIPE.
SOME OF THE EXOTICS THAT CAN BE USED;
ATEMOYA, CANISTEL, SOUR SOP,
RED BANANA, MAMEY, MANGO OR GUAVA.

Red Curry, Grapefruit and Guava sauce

Serves: 8

Guavas are found growing wild all around the Caribbean and Florida. Uglifruit can be substituted for grapefruit-if it is available and will make this recipe even better.

Ingredients:

1	tbs.	Extra-virgin olive oil
4	tbs.	Shallots, finely diced
1	qt.	Pink grapefruit juice
4	oz.	Dry vermouth
1 1/3	tbs.	Sugarcane syrup
1/2	each	Vanilla bean, scraped
1	cup	Chicken demi-glace
1	lb.	Guava pulp
As needed		Salt and pepper, 5:1 ratio
1/2	oz.	Red curry paste
As needed		Cornstarch and water, slurry

> **Hints:**
> A recipe that is sure to delight all. Even if you don't like grapefruit juice (like myself) try this one. This recipe "bursts" with excitement on the palate.

Instructions:

Sweat the shallots in the oil until translucent. Add the grapefruit juice and dry vermouth and cook over high heat. Then add the vanilla and sugarcane syrup. Let reduce down to 1/3 original volume. Add the demi and guava pulp reducing the volume again by half. Season and flavor. Add the cornstarch to thicken if necessary.

Nappe the bottom of the plate with the sauce and set fillet of fish on top.

Use for salmon, wahoo, pompano, dolphin or any flavorful fish. It can also be used to glaze pork.

Exotic Fruit Sauce

Serves: 4

Cherimoya has the luxurious taste and texture of vanilla pudding with a hint of cream and pineapple. It is perfect when combined with lighter tasting seafood selections.

Ingredients:

1	cup	Chardonnay
1	qt.	Orange juice
2	each	Bay leaf, crush roughly
2	tbs.	Shallots, finely chopped
3	tbs.	Sugar
3	oz.	Rice wine vinegar
2	each	Cherimoya, skinned, de-seed, * SEE NOTES

Hints:
The addition of whole butter will enrich the sauce and make it smoother for the palate.

Instructions:

ALWAYS use a stainless steel, heavy bottomed pan for recipes like this. It will keep the sauce looking bright and not an off grey color.

Reduce the orange juice with the shallots and bay leaf over high heat to a glaze. Add the wine and vinegar and reduce again to 1/3 of the original volume. Flavor with sugar to cut the concentrated bitterness. Mix in the cherimoya. By cutting in half and squeezing the pulp from skin, remove the seeds and puree the whole batch. Let simmer for five minutes so the flavors can meld. Strain and keep sauce warm till needed.

Notes:
Various **other** *exotic fruits* can be used as a replacement or in addition to this recipe.

Use anything from:
Lichee
Mango
Mamey
White sapote
Etc…

Guava B.B.Q. basting sauce

Serves: 8

This sauce shouldn't be confused with the other Guava B.B.Q sauce.

Ingredients:
1	cup	Guava paste
6	tbs.	Cider vinegar
1/4	cup	Dark rum
1/4	cup	Tomato paste
1/4	cup	Lime juice
1	tbs.	Soy sauce
2	teas.	Ketchup
2	teas.	Worcestershire
2	tbs.	Onions, fine chopped
1	tbs.	Ginger, fine chopped
2	each	Garlic kernels, smashed
1/2	each	Scotch bonnet pepper
As needed		Salt and pepper

Hints:
Guavas are found in various colors including yellow, pale yellow and green. All have a sweet, slightly sour gritty flesh ranging from white to salmon pink in color. Available from spring to fall. Hold at room temperature to ripen.

Instructions:
Mix all and cook over medium heat until well reduced. Mix evenly with a hand blender. Brush ribs while roasting.

Spicy Guava glaze

Serves: 8-10

Ingredients:
1	qt.	Guava juice
20	oz.	Roasted chicken demi-glace
1	cup	Chardonnay
3	oz.	Balsamic vinegar
1/2	each	Vanilla bean
1/2	cup	Orange blossom honey
1	teas.	Red curry paste
As needed		Salt and pepper, 5:1 ratio

Hints:
This an all-purpose glaze and can be used for basting cooked meats or blasting culinary creations. The subtle taste of the fruit will come thorough.

Con't on the next page

INSTRUCTIONS:
REDUCE GUAVA JUICE OVER HIGH HEAT UNTIL THE VOLUME IS REDUCED BY HALF. ADD THE WINE AND CHICKEN DEMI GLACE. REDUCE SAUCE VOLUME AGAIN BY HALF. ADD THE FLAVORINGS AND SPICES. ADD HONEY AND LET COOK UNTIL IT COATS THE BACK OF A WOODEN SPOON (NAPPE CONSISTENCY). POUR INTO JARS AND STORE OR USE RIGHT AWAY.

USE FOR:
     PORK, CHICKEN, BEEF, VEAL, RABBIT, QUAIL AND ALMOST ANY OTHER TYPE OF GAME MEAT. USE AS A SHELLAC TO COAT THESE MEATS WHILE THEY ARE COOKING ON THE GRILL. PAINT ONTO THE OUTSIDE OF THE FOODS AS IT COOKS, USING A **ROSEMARY OR THYME HERB BUNDLE AS YOUR BRUSH**.

JABOTICABA GLAZE
SERVES: 8-10

THIS FRUIT IS GREAT FOR USE ON LIGHTER SEAFOOD SELECTIONS. IT TASTES SIMILAR TO A MUSCADINE GRAPE. FOR A SUBSTITUTION, TRY A DARK GRAPE.

INGREDIENTS:

2	TBS.	OLIVE OIL
3	OZ.	SHALLOTS, CHOPPED FINE
1	QT.	JABOTICABA, CLEANED
1/2	CUP	MIRIN
2	OZ.	RICE WINE VINEGAR
4	OZ.	CHICKEN STOCK, DEMI-REDUCED
1/4	TEAS.	VANILLA, THE REAL STUFF
1/2	CUP	GUARAPO JUICE
1/2	TEAS.	SALT & PEPPER, 5:1 RATIO

HINTS:
I HAVE USED THIS FRUIT SUCCESSFULLY FOR MANY YEARS IN SAUCES, PUREES, VINAIGRETTES, ETC.... SEASONS VARY, BUT I HAVE HARVESTED THEM AS MANY AS FOUR TIMES A YEAR.

INSTRUCTIONS:
GET THE A STAINLESS STEEL POT VERY HOT. ADD OIL AND VERY QUICKLY SAUTE THE SHALLOTS. ADD FRUIT AND TOSS LIGHTLY. SMASH THE FRUIT WITH A SPOON. ADD THE NEXT THREE INGREDIENTS AND EXTRACT AS MUCH JUICE FROM THE BERRIES AS POSSIBLE. ADD THE STOCK AND RAPIDLY BOIL TO REDUCE THE VOLUME OF LIQUID BY HALF. FLAVOR AND SEASON TO TASTE. MASHING THE FRUIT TO EXTRACT JUICE, YOU SHOULD REDUCE THIS LIQUID BY HALF AGAIN AND ADD THE GUARAPO NEXT. SIMMER UNTIL SLIGHTLY THICKENED. STRAIN.

     I DO NOT USE *JABOTICABA* OFTEN IN THIS BOOK BECAUSE OF ITS RARITY IN GROCERY MARKETS.

Lemongrass and Soursop sauce

Serves: 8-10

Soursop is popular in the Caribbean. Rough looking green exterior with soft spikes. Once you taste the pulp inside, you won't question it's look anymore.

Ingredients:

3/4	lb.	Lemongrass, rough cut
1	qt.	Soursop, chunks, de-seeded
1/2	qt.	Chardonnay wine
1	each	Bay leaf
3	oz.	Shallots, fine
As needed		Salt and pepper, 5:1 ratio
1/4	cup	Corn syrup
1/4	cup	Pink peppercorns

Hints: Use on any grilled fish. Excellent with scallops.

Instructions:

Mix all in a heavy bottomed pot. Heat over a high flame and reduce volume by 3/4. Strain, add the corn syrup and seasonings. Nappe fish with the sauce and garnish with the pink peppercorns.

Mango beurre blanc

Serves: 8

Splash on all seafood dishes, particularly on full-flavored fish.

Ingredients:

1	tbs.	Olive oil
2	tbs.	Shallots, finely chopped
4	oz.	Chardonnay
2	oz.	Mango vinegar
1	cup	Mango puree
1	each	Bay leaf, bruised
3	oz.	Cream, heavy
2	oz.	Cold butter chips
As needed		Salt & pepper, 5:1 ratios
As needed		Cornstarch and water slurry

Hints: This recipe, although great, is not within the "Spa" guidelines like most of my recipes.

Instructions:

Sweat (cook slowly in oil) shallots in non-reactive stainless steel sauce pan. Add the wine and the vinegar. Let reduce over high heat to 1/3 original volume. Add the mango puree. Let simmer and reduce again by half. Add the cream and let simmer again until reduced by half again. Thicken if needed. Off heat add the whole butter. Season as needed. Hold warm.

Sprouted Mustard Seed sauce

Serves: 10

From the French Caribbean. See hints first.

Ingredients:

2	TBS.	Mustard seeds, see hints
As needed		Paper towels, dampened
1	QT.	Demi-glace, flavored with
1	OZ.	Madeira wine or 2 oz. dark rum
1	TBS.	Pommery grainy mustard
1	TEAS.	Thyme
As needed		Salt and pepper, 5:1 ratio
To taste		Honey

Hints:
Wet paper towels and lay the seeds on top. Let shells soften and sprout over the next 2-3 days in the refrigerator.

Instructions:

Let seeds sit for three days. As they sprout, the shell softens and becomes edible. Flavor increases dramatically. Add seeds and the rest of the ingredients to a saucepan and season as needed. Reduce volume of sauce over the flame to thicken.

After you bite into the first softened seed and taste the "zing" of a sprouted seed, you will understand why this recipe is in this book. Use for pork, lamb chops or veal loin roast.

Orange-Maple-Allspice glaze

Serves: 10

Shellac fillets of salmon, dolphin, wahoo, pompano and snappers before and after cooking.

Ingredients:

5	EACH	Allspice berries, crushed
1/2	CUP	Maple syrup
1/2	CUP	Orange juice concentrate
2	EACH	Orange juice and zest
4	EACH	Key lime juice and zest
2	EACH	Vanilla beans

Con't on the next page….

Hints:
You will find this glaze to be very important because it gives a sheen and flavor to baked fish.

INSTRUCTIONS:
Heat juices, syrup and the zest. Add the allspice and vanilla beans (split and scrape inside). Add the orange juice concentrate last. Simmer 30 minutes for the flavors to meld. Stir and crush the berries and vanilla beans with a wooden spatula as you mix. Strain.

Smoked Orange sauce
Serves: 10

INGREDIENTS:

12	each	Sweet oranges, Navel, Valencia, etc…
As needed		Wood chips, first soak in water for 20 minutes
1	tbs.	Seafood Creole seasonings, see recipe page 83
2	oz.	Honey
1/2	cup	Rice wine vinegar
1	cup	Chablis
2	oz.	Rum
1	pt.	Chicken demi glace, well reduced
1	oz.	Orange juice, concentrate
4	oz.	Orange juice
1	tbs.	Salt, or to taste
As needed		Cornstarch and water slurry

INSTRUCTIONS:
Soak the wood chips. Heat the chips over the white hot char-grill coals. Smoke halved oranges well until browned and perfumed in a covered charcoal grill. Over high heat, reduce volume of the chicken demi, wine and vinegar reduce volume of sauce by two-thirds. Squeeze out as much juice as you can from the oranges. Add the rest of the ingredients. Reduce by half. Thicken if necessary with a cornstarch / water slurry.

Fire-spice Papaya B.B.Q. sauce
Serves: 10

INGREDIENTS:

1	cup	B.B.Q. sauce, your recipe
1	cup	Papaya pulp
1/2	cup	Key lime juice
10	stalks	Cilantro, chopped
As needed		Salt
To taste		Honey
1	each	Scotch bonnet peppers, chopped
1/3	teas.	Vanilla, see recipe page

Con't on the next page…..

HINTS:

Scotch Bonnets are very hot peppers. On the Islands, a dish can never be too hot.

INSTRUCTIONS:
WARM THE B.B.Q SAUCE. ADD THE REST OF THE INGREDIENTS TO THIS SAUCE AND WITH A MIXING WAND STIR AND BLEND COMPLETELY. LET SIMMER FOR 5 MINUTES SO THE FLAVORS TO MELD. STRAIN.

YOU COULD USE CALAMONDINE OR UGLI-FRUIT JUICE AS A SUBSTITUTE FOR THE LIME JUICE.
USE WITH GRILLED CHICKEN BREAST OR CRITTER FRITTERS ON PAGE 44

SIMPLE PASSIONFRUIT SAUCE
SERVES: 8

THIS IS THE RECIPE YOU WANT TO USE FOR THAT FRESH YELLOWTAIL SNAPPER YOU JUST CAUGHT ON YOUR KEY WEST VACATION.

INGREDIENTS:
1	TBS.	OLIVE OIL
2	EACH	SHALLOTS, FINELY CHOPPED
1/2	CUP	ORANGE, JUICE AND IT'S ZEST (1 TBS.)
1/2	CUP	SUGARCANE JUICE (REDUCED TO SYRUP)
1	CUP	PASSIONFRUIT PULP PUREE
AS NEEDED.		CORNSTARCH, IN WATER.

INSTRUCTIONS:
SAUTE SHALLOTS WITH OIL. ADD THE SUGARCANE JUICE, ORANGE JUICE, AND ZEST, CARAMELIZE LIGHTLY. REDUCE BY HALF VOLUME. ADD THE PASSIONFRUIT PUREE. ADD THE CORNSTARCH TO THICKEN SLIGHTLY.

PEACH-ORANGE COULIS
SERVES: 15

INGREDIENTS:
2	OZ.	KEY LIME JUICE
1	CUP	CHARDONNAY
2	OZ.	SHALLOTS, FINELY DICED
2	CUPS	PEACHES, PUREED
2	OZ.	ORANGE JUICE CONCENTRATE
2	CUPS	CHICKEN DEMI GLAZE, WELL REDUCED
2	OZ.	ORANGE BLOSSOM HONEY
1/2	TEAS.	ROASTED CHIPOTLE PEPPER (GROUND)

CON'T ON THE NEXT PAGE....

INSTRUCTIONS:
PUREE PEACHES WITH THE WINE, LIME JUICE AND SHALLOTS. HEAT TO A RAPID BOIL AND REDUCE TO A THICKER, SYRUPY CONSISTENCY. ADD THE STOCK AND THE REST OF THE LIQUIDS. REDUCE AGAIN OVER HIGH HEAT TO A THICKENED CONSISTENCY. ADD THE SEASONS. STRAIN AND KEEP WARM FOR LATER USE.

YOU CAN ENRICH THIS SAUCE WITH 3 OZ. OF *WHOLE BUTTER,*
BUT IT LOOSES ITS SPA CUISINE PARAMETERS.

PO-POO SAUCE

SERVES: 25

USE AS A MARINADE AND/OR DIPPING SAUCE. FREEZE IN SMALLER BATCHES AND DEFROST WHEN NEEDED. THIS SAUCE WORKS WELL WITH ALL FOODS THAT NEED A DISTINCTIVE FLAVOR BOOST.

INGREDIENTS:

2	LBS.	YOUNG BEETS, PEELED, QUARTERED
3	OZ.	RED WINE
1	QT.	RED WINE VINEGAR
2	OZ.	SHALLOTS, CHOPPED
2	EACH	BAY LEAF, CRUMBLED
2	OZ.	GINGER, FINE CHOPPED
3	OZ.	RASPBERRY VINEGAR
2	LBS.	RASPBERRIES, FRESH PICKED
6	OZ.	ORIENTAL B.B.Q. SAUCE, "AH-SU" (AT GOURMET GROCER)
6	OZ.	HOISEN SAUCE
4	OZ.	HONEY

INSTRUCTIONS:
BOIL BEETS UNTIL SOFT IN THE NEXT FIVE INGREDIENTS. REDUCE THE LIQUID VOLUME BY HALF AND THEN ADD THE NEXT TWO INGREDIENTS. USE A HAND IMMERSION MIXER WHEN SAUCE IS HOT AND ADD THE HOISEN AND THE "AH-SU" SAUCE. REMOVE FROM THE HEAT AND ADD THE HONEY. COOL.

HINTS:

JUNE AND JULY IS RASPBERRY SEASON. TAKE ADVANTAGE OF THE JUST PICKED FLAVORS WHILE YOU CAN.

USE FOR:

SHELLACING RIBS, AND WILD GAME.

Soursop sauce

Serves: 15

This fruit's rich, aromatic custardy flesh will tantalize your palate. Great with delicately flavored seafood like grilled scallops.

Ingredients:

2	each	Soursop (about two pounds each) cleaned, deseeded
6	oz.	Chardonnay wine
5	each	Lime juice
2	each	Bay leaf
1/2	teas.	White peppercorns, crushed, fine
8	oz.	Cream
1/2	lb	Butter, softened
1	teas.	Real vanilla extract, use freshly made

Instructions:

Heat first five ingredients in a stainless steel pot until half the original volume is reached. Add the cream and reduce again by one-half. Add the softened butter. Flavor and season.

Starfruit essence

Serves: 50

Ingredients:

1	liter	White vermouth
4	each	Starfruit, peeled, chopped
10	each	Black peppercorns
2	each	Bay leaf, bruised
2	1" piece	Orange peel
1	inch piece	Lemon peel

Instructions:

Mix all and let marinate atop a shelf overnight. Remove and distill, as in the recipe on page 111 for the Thai essence. Bottle and place in refrigerator until ready to use.

Hints:

The delicate taste of this five pointed tropical fruit is concentrated to the extreme. It's a flavor booster for sauces, sprayed atop cooked seafood for added flavor enhancement, and can be used as a flavor builder for scented rice products.

Thai "Spritz" ~ Essence

Serves: 50

Ingredients:

3	stalks	Lemongrass
6	each	Habenero chilies
24	each	Cilantro stems
2	tbs.	Black peppercorns
2	each	Bay leaf
3	1" pieces	Fresh ginger, bruised with the back of a knife.
1	liter	Vodka

Hints:

This recipe will astound you with its flavor.

Instructions:

Mix all and cover. Place on a shelf for two days. Follow the rest of the distilling instructions. The final liquid will be placed inside a spray bottle and squirted over foods of your choosing to give them a special "kick-in-the-pants".

Set up a distilling chamber......
You need 1 pot that a metal bowl can sit atop and a smaller bowl can fit inside (on the bottom of the inside of the boiling pot). Place the mixture (recipe above) in the larger pot. Place the smaller bowl inside atop the mixture (inside the large pot). Place the large bowl atop the pot and fill this bowl with ice. Now heat the mixture (with the assembly in place) until the liquid barely reaches a simmer (about 100 degrees). Let the mixture evaporate completely over a medium heat. As this mixture evaporates, it collects on the cooler bowl's bottom (filled with ice) it cools the condensed vapors and that liquid drips into the bowl inside the pot. The essence that is collected is pure "Thai" flavor-extract. Cover quickly and save in the refrigerator until ready for service.

TO USE: Spray atop foods for a quick essence boost to the plate, add to a sauce or compote of fruits.

Now you can use this same process to distill the "real-vanilla" recipe to concentrate flavors.

Smoked Yellow Tomato sauce

Serves: 10

Please don't use hickory wood for this recipe.

Ingredients:
1	lb.	Yellow tomatoes, halved
1	cup	Wood chips (I prefer Florida oak)
3	bags	Green tea leaves
1/2	cup	Shallots, fine
2	tbs.	Garlic, fine
2	each	Bay leaf
1	qt.	Chicken demi glace, half reduce

Instructions:
Soak the wood chips for 30 minutes in water. Heat the chips atop hot coals (with the lid shut) until they start to smoke. Place halved tomatoes above the chips on the grill grates. Let smoke five minutes covered. Then spread the tea leaves over grey coals and close lid quickly allowing to smoke another 10 minutes. Keep the fire just hot enough to keep the wood smoking. Heat the chicken stock, flavor and season. Add the tomatoes and puree by blending with a hand held mixer. After blending, let simmer 30 minutes for the flavors to meld. Strain and keep warm until needed.

Use for roasted poultry, meats and some stronger tasting seafood.

Vanilla, the real stuff

60 applications

Ingredients:
1	qt.	Vodka
6	each	Vanilla beans
As needed		Sunlight

Instructions:
Split the beans and scrape the inside with the back of a knife. Place the vanilla specs into the liquor with beans. Place all in glass bottle and set on window sill for three days. Strain out the beans thorough a fine wire mesh. To concentrate this flavor, use the Thai essence distillation process recipe (that is on previous page).

Hints:

Beans will flavor the liquor and you will have a excellent vanilla extract.

Shells and Scales

There are rivers in Florida that run so pure and clean they bare names of the "Blue Run", "Rainbow", "Silver" and "Crystal".

HEALTH BENEFITS OF EATING FISH

Fish and seafood are nutrient rich foods that are readily available to most Americans. They are a good source of high-quality lean protein and are rich in many micro-nutrients, such as unsaturated fatty acids, vitamins, and minerals.

In addition, they are generally lower in saturated fatty acids (a risk factor that most meats have that produce problems with heart diseases) than other protein foods.

Consequently, many health organizations concerned about the relationships between diet and health recommend that most Americans increase their consumption of fish.

Seafood Hints....

Buying fish

You can't create a great tasting meal with poor quality fish. Judging a fish's quality is of utmost importance. Umami is a Japanese translation meaning quality at its peak. Fish is freshly harvested, handled by skillful fishermen, stored in perfect conditions and sold to you perfectly fresh.

Umami means it has an immediate and compelling appeal to your senses. Scales are intact, gills are bright red and have a glistening shimmer. Fresh fish is firm and resilient to the touch, smells clean, and is almost sweet. Smell the body cavity...it should not smell like fish! A fresh fish will have bright eyes that are not sunken. Bruised fish will show up in the fillet as discolorations and quickly spoil. The flesh surrounding the bruise will be soft and mushy.

Cut fresh fish will have a bright appearance with a truly intense hue. A fish that has been handled well will show that quality through these factors. As they begin to age they might be treated with a chemical STP-sodium tripolyphosphate. It is used to retard bacteria growth. Although useful, these additives leave a chemical taste.

Another quality loss in cut fish is its drip lost. Drip lost is the continual loss of moisture from the individual protein cells. This loss of moisture and cell collapsing leaves the fillets soft and without firmness. At this point fish has little quality, and when cooked the texture is dry without any meaningful taste.

FISH USAGE

Understanding that there is a certain use for each fish and the reasons why they are prepared in a certain style, has been a problem for most of us. There is a specific cooking practice for every fish.

We bake, steam, broil, grill and poach certain fish because of their flesh (we will call it their character). Some characteristics can tolerate one cookery treatment and wither with another. Some fish take well to grilling, (like dolphin, tuna, wahoo or snapper) some don't (like flat fishes, flounders). If fish is to be grilled properly, a high temperature is needed. Because fatty fish have a higher moisture content from the amount of fat interspersed within the character, they can be grilled with reasonable ease. Also, many of these varieties of fish have a character that constricts as it cooks. The fatty fish's character fibers (flakes) are generally much thicker than leaner fish. Flaking of the flesh is caused by the fat melting out of the fillet, and their character falls apart. Generally all high fat fish can be cooked with the high heat methods (broiled, grilled, baked). Most of the fish from South Florida are of the high fat content type and are perfectly suited for these types of cooking treatments. This is why most of my recipes call for grilling.

JUDGING FISH QUALITY

There are many considerations to evaluate when inspecting fresh seafood products. When judging freshness always look for:
On whole fish-clear eyes and red gills.
On fillets-tight-firm flesh,
> no discolorations,
> no butchering mistakes,
> no parasites,
> no excess water in packing (a sign that it might have been a frozen product),
> only a fresh sea-air scent

Each fish has its own characteristics. As experience builds, you will be able to catch all the blemishes that culinary professionals look for when judging fresh fish. Education and experience are your best guides when judging quality.

South Florida Aquaculture

It is a beautiful sight riding the country back roads lined with heavily laden mango trees after the disaster of Hurricane Andrew a decade ago. After this hurricane, the tropical fruit industries' production was pushed back more than three years. This could also be said about our fledgling South Florida aquaculture industry. The South Florida Aquaculture Center is our first, and so far the only commercial fish farm facility selling Stripe bass to chefs.

When Andrew blew thorough, it almost removed the South Florida Aquaculture center with its passing. Two days after the storm left and the waters receded, the Stripe bass ranchers came back to find most of their crop of the hybrid bass and the buildings blown across the Everglades. The production at that time was at 500 pounds of hybrid Stripe bass a week. While evidence of Andrew's presence is still seen, rebuilding is more prevalent. Everybody had a feeling of rebirth after the storm. The only thing to do after a storm like Andrew is re-build, because there wasn't much left to reconstruct.

As we swerve to avoid one of South Florida's deadliest residents, a four foot "Coral" snake warming itself on the abandoned road, eagles, egrets, and many varieties of heron greet us as we arrive. The people I have talked to (and later started buying from) are knowledgeable and committed to their ranch. As they put it, "the more fish we raise and harvest, the more fish are left in our oceans."

The hybrid of the "White" and "Stripe" bass are kept in 200'x20' above-ground tanks which occupy an area the size of a couple football fields. As many as 3000 full-sized, two pound fish are held in each of these giant tanks. Because of their growth rate, most of the stock at this facility is still smaller fish. The warm year-round water (70-72 degree) from the underground aquifers makes for ideal growing conditions for this species. After they reach the 1 pound size, each fish will put on a quarter pound per month.

Our only farm raised seafood commodity is harvested and shipped within 24 hours-to local chefs. This hybrid is extremely adapted to the constant warm weather conditions and is thought to be one of the finest farm-raised fish of the future. This variety of fish, high in Omega-3 fatty acids, will excite even the most experienced palate.

SHELLFISH,
is for Florida seafood lovers....and, there is always a party!

"Appalachicola" oysters are the best in Florida. This area has been harvesting these prized crustacean for generations. The Oystermen are members of a society that has been around for hundreds of years. The Appalachicola oyster is so prolific that there are third generation oystermen still working the oyster beds that their grandparents started in the early 1900's.

Being a oysterman is not only a profession, it is a lifestyle. It means getting up before the sun everyday, already fishing for hours before many us even see our first cup of coffee. On any given day you can see flat-hauled, shallow-running skiffs scattered all over the bay that forms the mouth of the Appalachicola River.

This is the best place in the nation for harvesting oysters because of the water flows in and out of this river basin. The entire water-encircled township revolves around the harvesting of this mollusk. Their restaurants feature the use of oysters for all sorts of dinner items.

There is nothing better to a true oysterman than a "sweet" half shell. The term "sweet" is a local term to tell diners that the oysters were harvested when there was a heavy fresh water flow out of the river and it pushed the bay "salt" water out of this harvesting area. The oyster filters water for their food. As the fresh water goes through the mollusk, it cleans the briny flavors away. Appalach (the way local people refer to Appalachicola, Florida) oysters are harder to find outside the West Coast of Florida, but it is worth every effort to obtain Florida's best.

On the first week of November there is a week-long event centering around the harvesting of these oysters. The "Florida Seafood Festival" is the state's oldest maritime exhibit for local seafood and features parades, pirating regalia and local food~of course. It is held on the streets of this "Key West" reminiscent township of Appalach.

"Indian River" Blue crab are the largest I have found in Florida. The Indian River-Blue crab is a South Florida's favorite. The waters of the Indian River are fed by underground salt springs that originate deep within a purifying limestone bed that makes up most of Florida's geological substructure. The Blue crabs make their way down the river from the river's mouth that adjoins the Atlantic Ocean. The crabs travel in fresh water so long they turn sweeter-like the oysters from Appalacah do when they are flushed by the sweet fresh water of the Appalachicola River.

"Titusville" Rock shrimp are an odd specialty product popularized by a few chefs in South Florida. I have been using these lobster-like shrimp since the 1970's. Their rock-hard shells give them their names. It is a difficult product to utilize, but their taste is a sought after delicacy. The flavor of a Rock shrimp is a cross between lobster and shrimp.

"Jacksonville" shrimp probably the best fresh "white" shrimp you will ever taste. The sands (where the shrimp live) of the Gulfstream are the whitest and most pure right off the coast of Jacksonville. The sea scent of a freshly sauteed Jacksonville shrimp will permeate all your senses. The Key West Pink shrimp is right behind this one as one of my favorites. The pinks are just a little more briny than the Whites from Jacksonville.

"Spiny Lobsters" is another sought after South Florida commodity. Found all over South Florida, but typically caught in the Caribbean Sea fed waters of the Florida Keys. These spiny lobster are unlike their northern cousins. They don't have large frontal claws like the Maine lobster. The warm water lobster tastes and cooks up like it's cousin, but its texture is different. Called "Bugs" in the Caribbean where I have lived, they are caught in almost any rocky shoreline. If you dive at night, you can see them scurrying across the bottom of the sea floor. Their Caribbean namesake comes from the description of what it is like to turn on the lights of the kitchen at night and the bugs scatter and hide.

The "Annual Florida Keys Seafood Festival" is an event that showcases local seafood of the local commercial fishing fleet. Each year local fishermen offer visitors a variety of seafood for sale and to partake in from carnival-like booths. There are turtle races, crab races and of course, bar crawls.

"Bahamian" Conch. Most of the conch that is harvested in the Bahamas and will make it's way to Florida. The Key West production of conch is illegal now to protect the species, so the Bahamian conch is the next best choice. Although other parts of the Caribbean harvest conch, I like in the British Virgin Islands, but it is rarely distributed outside that region.

"Pan-Handle" Bay Scallop. Scallop harvesting is a tradition in all Panhandle communities of north Florida. Floating behind a skiff and picking up scallops as you waft over seaweed beds, has been a ritual for families in Florida for decades. These little jet propelled mollusks make their homes in the shallow water, grassy seaweed beds of the Gulf of Mexico. You can look out across any shallow water bay or harbour expanse and see off in the distance the tiny specs of boats dotting the bay. Seeing these summertime harvesters is so common during the scallop season that only a very large storm would keep scallop-ers off the water.

In the northern counties of Florida "scallop" season is looked forward to like the Fourth of July celebrations in Washington D.C. There are many two or three day long festivals that occur every year to celebrate another scallop season.

Just before the Fourth of July every year, the scallops season opens in North Florida. In the middle of the three month season there is a scallops festival in Port of St. Joe, Florida - a small town in between Panama City and Appalachicola, that attracts visitors from as far away as Atlanta.

At this same time of year, a smaller event happen to celebrate local seafood, it is the "Boggy Bay Mullet-Throwing" contest. And it is exactly what it sounds like. Participants line up to see who can throw a five pound Mullet the farthest down the road. Participants have to have the skills of an Olympian shot-putter and a fishmonger at the famous Pike's Fish Market in Seattle.

"Tampa Bay" Clam these giant chowder clams can be easily be found in the shallows all over the Tampa Bay region. Too large for anything but chopping and stewing in a chowder, they have a dense flavor to them.

Ruskin (Tampa-area) Seafood Festival is held during the first week of November. This festival is the largest Tampa community event - with over 18,000 in attendance. It is where seafood lovers feast on lobster, oysters, clams, grouper, shrimp and the ever-present slow-smoked Southern specialty, mullet.

STONERS

The sun is just now peeking out from behind the horizon on this blustery 15th day of October. The waves pound the skiff as we cruise up to the next buoy. As we strain to pull the long seaweed-covered tethered line, the blue-green algae covered wooden crab trap is hoisted into the boat. Several months of strategic placement and baiting lead up to this brief moment of anticipation. Stone crabs, Florida's most prized crustacean, is today being harvested all over the State.

The season for harvesting began early this morning. By 8:00 AM we already made our rounds and have our catch for the day. As soon as we hit the shore, the legs are separated by size. Some of the harvested claws (only one is harvested off each crab) weigh more than a pound. The sorted claws are placed in a very large basket and lifted in and out of the boiling cooking vat via a crane.

The Vat, 30 gallons of boiling water, has been ready for hours awaiting our return this morning. After shocking in a ice water bath to stop their cooking, the claws are ready to eat. It just so happens that the mustard sauce is already here in this makeshift kitchen and we enjoy a breakfast that makes a memory for years to come. When the legs have chilled enough, they are rushed to the local fishmongers. Fish markets all over Florida have been waiting for these shipments.

Stone crabs have been anxiously awaited for by crustacean lovers since the close of the previous season. Although we have a multitude of other crustaceans harvested in Florida waters, loyalty to these tasty morsels runs deep in every Stone crab admirer.

Crustacean zealots rejoice, this is the start of another Stone crab season.

CHARACTERISTICS OF COMMONLY USED FISH

Species:	Texture	Flake	Tastes*	Flavor profile
Grouper	THICKER CHEW	LARGE FLAKE	LIGHT OIL	MEDIUM FLAVORED
Seabass	VERY TENDER	MEDIUM FLAKE	RICH OIL	HIGH FLAVOR
Salmon	MEATY-THICK	MEDIUM FLAKE	RICH OIL	HIGH FLAVOR
Mahi Mahi	VERY MEATY	LARGE FLAKE	SLIGHT OIL	FULL FLAVOR
Wahoo	MEATY BITE	STEAK-LIKE	HIGH IN OIL	VERY FLAVORFUL
Cobia	MEATY	STEAK-LIKE	HIGH IN OIL	MEDIUM FLAVOR
Yellowtail	VERY TENDER	SMALL	VERY LIGHT	NEAR NEUTRAL
Yellowfin	PLIABLE	STEAK-LIKE	RICH TASTES	FULL FLAVOR
Bigeye Tuna	FIRM-COOKED	LARGE FLAKE	RICHER	FULL FLAVOR
Pompano	FIRM	SMALL FLAKE	RICH	MEDIUM FLAVOR
Escolar, White Tuna	SOFT	VERY TENDER	DISTINCTIVE	FULL, RICH FLAVOR
Swordfish	FIRM	STEAK-LIKE	SOLID FLAVOR	MILD FLAVOR
Pumpkin Swordfish	SOFT	STEAK-LIKE	SWEETER	GOOD FLAVOR
Halibut	FIRM	SOFT-STEAK	HIGH FLAVOR	MEDIUM FLAVOR
Sole/ Flounder	SOFT	VERY TENDER	LIGHT	VERY LIGHT
Caribbean Lobster	FIRM	DENSER MEAT	LIGHT OIL	HIGHLY FLAVORFUL
Scallops	VERY SOFT	NONE	HIGHLY TASTY	LIGHT-NEUTRAL
Shrimp	FIRM	NONE	MILD TO MEDIUM	IODINE/SALT
Oysters	SOFT	NONE	SALTY SWEET	HIGH
Conch	FIRM	NONE	SWEET	HIGH
Mussels	FIRM	NONE	SWEET	HIGH

Notes:
* = denotes Omega three fatty acids, proven to be a healthy choice for all consumers.

Banana Bass

Serves: 4

Ingredients:

4	8 oz.	Stripe bass fillets
1	Tbs.	Lipstick oil (annatto oil) see page 143
Pinch		Salt and pepper, 5:1 ratio
1	each	Yellow tomato, chopped
1/2	cup	Super-sweet pineapple, chopped
1/3	each	Roasted red bell pepper, diced
1	Tbs.	Shallots, diced finely
4	each	Banana leaves, grilled

Hints: When wrapped around fillets, the grilled banana leaves give the entire dish a perfumed aroma.

Instructions:
Preheat the BBQ grill. Rub the filets with the oil and season. Mix the next four ingredients in a bowl and keep until needed. Toast the leaves over flames on the grill. Lay the leaves out on a work space. Spread the fruit and tomato compote over the center portion of the leaves. Place the seasoned fillet on top. Fold up the banana leaves into a envelope and secure with butcher's twine. Place the fillets near the flame (but not directly over the flame itself) on the baking rack of the grill and close the lid. Bake the fillets for about 10 minutes. Unwrap, and enjoy the fruit perfumed seafood.

Smoked Cobia with Papaya salsa

Serves: 6

Smokyiness is just the right "taste-variance" needed to make this dish special

Ingredients:

2 1/2	lbs.	Cobia fillets, 7 oz.
2	cups	Florida Oak chips - Soaked 20 minutes in water
2	cups	Papaya salsa, see recipe 50
1 1/2	cups	Smoky tomato sauce, see recipe 112
As needed		Creole seafood spice, see recipe page 83

Instructions:
Heat grill and let coals turn gray. Make the sauce and salsa. Season the fillets. Toss the wet chips over the hot coals and then place the cobia on the oiled grill, not directly over the hottest coals, and close the lid. Cook about 10 minutes. Fillets should be lightly colored. Place fillets atop the smoky tomato sauce on plate and surround with the salsa scattered about randomly.

Souffled Fish Fingers

Serves: 8-10

Ingredients:

4	each	Eggs, separated
4	oz.	Beer
1/2	teas.	Baking powder
3/4	box	Cornstarch
1/3	cup	Flour + 1 cup for dredging
1	teas.	Powdered ginger
1	teas.	Onion powder
1	teas.	Garlic powder
1/4	teas.	Mustard powder
1/3	teas.	5-spice powder
1/2	teas.	Salt
1	oz.	Soy sauce
1	teas.	Yellow food coloring
1 3/4	lbs.	Grouper, corvina, cod, cut into fingers-size pieces

Instructions:

Mix the dry ingredients. Whip the whites separately until stiff. Mix beer, soy sauce and the yolks and then add to the dry ingredients. Whip well to break up all the clumps. Fold in the whites. Toss the fingers in the other half the flour to coat, dredge through the batter. Slowly hand-dip into a deep fryer. Cook at 350 degrees until golden brown. Stir the fingers so they brown evenly. They should quickly rise to the top of the oil if the batter is made right.

Redlands Black Grouper

Serves: 6

The Redlands is a place of unknown acreage filled by tropical fruit groves. This recipe is similar to what is known in the islands as "Rundown".

Ingredients:

6	each	Black grouper fillets, about 7 oz. each
As needed		Seafood spice blend, see recipe page 85
1	each	Mango, chopped
2	each	Red bananas (diced)
12	each	Loquats, halved, de-seeded
2	each	Lime, juiced over top the fruit
1/4	cup	Triple sec
As needed		Salt and pepper, 5:1 ratio
2	oz.	Sweetened condensed milk
6	each	Mint, fresh, garni

Hints: This is a beautiful dish paired with an "oaky" Chardonnay

Instructions:

Mix the fruit and let macerate (soak) with the liquor for 2 hours. Season fillets. Place in baking pan and top with fruit. Bake for 10 minutes at 350 degrees, or until done. Scoop up the fish and layer on platter. Toss the fruit and pan juices in a saute pan and briefly heat to evaporate liquids. Add condensed milk. Season if necessary. Top the fillets with the fruit reduction. Let the sauce "Rundown - Mon!". Garnish with fresh mint cluster.

Florida Groupers: Red, Black, Nassau

Sofrito crusted Black Grouper

Serves: 4

HINTS:

You might need to add a little flour to make a more firm crust.

As an alternative, try cornmeal.

Ingredients:

4	8 oz. pcs.	Gulf black grouper
As needed		Salt and pepper
2	tbs.	Olive oil
1	bunch	Scallions, diced
1/2	cup	Assorted peppers, diced
2	each	Jalapenos, fine diced
4	each	Garlic
1/3	bunch	Parsley, chopped
1/2	bunch	Cilantro, chopped
1/4	cup	Dry vermouth
As needed		Flour (optional)

Instructions:

Season fillets of grouper. Then make the sofrito. Saute scallions and next 6 ingredients adding one at a time. Heat over low flame until all are soft. Coat the top the fish with this mixture. Bake at 350 degrees, about 11 minutes per inch of fillet thickness.

Use the smoked orange sauce, page 107 to compliment this dish.

Southwestern crusted Grouper

Serves: 6

Ingredients:

3	lbs.	Grouper, 8 oz. fillets
1	cup	Southwestern crust, see recipe on page 85
As needed		Olive Oil, extra-virgin
1/2	cup	Orange juice concentrate
3/4	cup	Mango beurre blanc, see recipe on page 105
3	cups	Papaya fruit salsa, see recipe page 50
2	cups	Green papaya kimchee, see recipe page 60

Instructions:

Paint top of the grouper fillets with orange juice concentrate. Sprinkle with the S.W. crust. Grill lightly and then finish cooking in the oven, for about 10 minutes. Sauce the bottom of the plate with the mango beurre blanc. Set the fillets atop some grilled veggies or potato souffle and surround with the sauce. Garnish the plate with a tropical fruit salsa and the kimchee.

Scallops with Starfruit Thai Crust

Serves: 4

Ingredients:

20	each	Scallops, under five to the pound size
As needed		Salt and pepper
As needed		Olive oil
1/2	teas.	Lemon juice
1	tbs.	Herb oil, see recipe page 135
20	piece	Pencil asparagus, blanched
1/2	cup	Onion crust, see recipe page 84
3	tbs.	Thai peanut seasons, found in Asian markets
1	oz.	Starfruit essence, see recipe page 110
2	oz.	Passionfruit sauce, see recipe page 108
1/3	teas.	Spikes seasoning, found at gourmet grocers

Instructions:

Marinate the scallops in a little lemon juice and salt and pepper. Set aside. Mark the blanched asparagus on a hot grill. Brush with the herb oil as they cook. Rub the grates of the grill with a little of the oil. Sear the scallops on the grill. Cook until opaque all the way thorough. Place a little passionfruit atop the seared scallops and sprinkle with the onion crust that has been mixed with the Thai peanut mix. Place the asparagus and scallops on the plate alternating each in a circular pattern-like hands on a clock. Drizzle a little of the oil over the asparagus. Drizzle a little of the passionfruit around the plate and the starfruit essence atop each scallop. Serve with a scoop of Sun-natured rice see recipe on page 178 in the center of the plate.

Grilled Scallops and Calamondin

Serves: 4

Ingredients:

20	each	Scallops, under 10 to the pound size
1/2	cup	Achiote vinaigrette, see recipe page 70
As needed		Oil, to brush the grill
As needed		Salt and pepper, 5:1 ratio
1	cup	Calamondin sauce, see recipe page 99

Instructions:

Marinate scallops in the vinaigrette for one hour. Heat coals to the grey point. Oil slats and place the seasoned scallops on them. After cooking, place on plate that has a nappe of the sauce.

Blackened Mango Seabass

Serves: 4

Ingredients:

2	LBS.	Seabass, cut into 8 oz. portions
1	EACH	Lemon, juiced
1 1/2	TBS.	Seafood creole spice, see recipe 83
2	CUP	Black bean and corn compote, see recipe page 165
1	EACH	Mango, peeled and fanned with a sharp knife
1/2	TEAS.	Creole seasoning
4	OZ.	Honey-orange blossom
12	OZ.	SoFlo Apple Cider sauce, see recipe on page 98
1	TBS.	Chipotle peppers, crushed to a fine dust
2	OZ.	Sherry vinegar
As needed		Oil, for searing in wok

Instructions:

After cutting seabass portions, season with the lemon. Sprinkle with a dusting of creole seasoning. Sear fillets quickly in a super-hot wok and then transfer to a baking sheet. Cook in a 375 degree oven until done. About 10 minutes per inch of fillet thickness. Set the mango (see below) atop the fillets.

For the sauce... Add the chipotle pepper dust to the Apple cider sauce - and use this to nappe fillets when done.

For mango garnish... Sear the mangos in a non-stick pan after sprinkling lightly with Creole seasoning. Remove from the pan and lay a top the fillets. Then add the honey to the pan and caramelize over high heat. Deglaze by adding the sherry vinegar and pour over the mangos after you place them a top the fish.

Garnish... Sprinkle the corn compote around the bottom of each plate. Place the seabass fillet in center of plate and nappe with a little more sauce.

Seared Scallops

Serves: 6

Ingredients:

3	LBS	Scallops, under 10 per pound size
5	TBS.	Seafood spice rub, see recipe page 85
2 1/4	CUPS	Spicy guava sauce, see recipe page 103
2	CUPS	Baby greens, loose pack
4	OZ.	Opal basil vinaigrette, see recipe page 73

Instructions:

Take the scallops and dip into the seafood spice rub dipping, only the flat ends into the rub. Sear in a hot wok, or hot cast iron skillet. Remove when lightly charred and finish cooking the scallops in 350 degree oven for about eight minutes until the centers are opaque. Give them a little squeeze, they should be just soft but not ridged-hard. Divide the scallops among plates. Coat plate (nappe) with red curry sauce, set scallops atop.

Garnish with a small baby greens salad, tossed in the opal basil vinaigrette.

Seabass with Chimichurri beurre blanc

Serves: 6

Ingredients:

3	lbs.	Seabass, 8 oz. portions
As needed		Salt & pepper
1	each	Lime juice
1	cup	Cornmeal
1	teas.	Chipotle, dust
1/2	teas.	Kosher salt
1	tbs.	Thyme
2	oz.	Olive oil
2	tbs.	Shallots, finely diced
10	each	Black peppercorns
1/2	cup	Sherry
2	oz.	Sherry wine vinegar
1	cup	Heavy cream
1/3	lb.	Butter
As needed		Salt & pepper
1/3	cup	Cilantro, fine cut, squeeze out moisture
4	tbs.	Herbena Chimi-churri, see recipe on page 83

Instructions:

Season seabass with salt and pepper and a squeeze or two of lime juice. Mix cornmeal with the chipotle dust, salt and thyme. Add the seabass into the cornmeal mix and coat well. Quickly saute and remove from the pan. Finish cooking in a 375 degree oven for up to 10 minutes per inch of the fish fillet. Wipe the pan out and sweat the shallots. Add the next three ingredients and reduce down to 1/5 the original volume. Don't use too large (wide at bottom) of a pan, or it will burn before reducing. Add the cream and reducing volume by half, stirring constantly. Add the butter in small chunks off the heat. Add the cilantro now. Keep warm, don't heat again. Season if necessary. Place the sauce on a plate and place the seabass atop. Dot the presentation with the Herbena Chimi-churri.

SEABASS WITH CHIMICHURRI BEURRE BLANC...SEE PREVIOUS PAGE
WOOD-GRILLED VEGGIES...PAGE 181
WASABI POTATOES...PAGE 179

GRILLED RACK OF SHRIMP, SEE PAGE 135

SESAME SEARED TUNA LOIN...PAGE 140

Thai Basil crusted Atlantic Snapper

Serves: 10

Ingredients:

1 1/2	oz.	Orange juice concentrate
1	tbs.	Tamari
1	tbs.	Sesame oil
1	teas.	Chili paste
1	bunch	Thai basil, found in oriental markets
1	oz.	Onion crust, see recipe page 84 using note on bottom
1/2	cup	Bread crumbs
1	teas.	Paprika
10	7 oz.	Red snapper fillets
20	oz.	Apricot-ginger glaze, see recipe page 95
13	sprigs	Mint, (10 for garnish)

Instructions:

Mix the first four ingredients together in a bowl. Dip the fillets into the marinade, marinating for up to 30 minutes ahead of time. Make the crust with the rest of the ingredients except the snapper and the glaze. After you remove fillets from marinade, place onto a baking sheet and sprinkle with the crust. Preheat the oven to 375 degrees. Place the pan in the oven on the middle rack. Bake the fillets seven minutes per inch of thickness (example...2 inch fillets would take about 13-14 minutes). The crust should brown to a deep golden color. Remove from oven and let rest for 3 minutes before moving to warm platter. Place the sauce on your serving plate and then top with the cooked fillets. Drizzle half the sauce over the fillets. Garnish with entire deep fried sprigs of mint.

Cornmeal crusted Shrimp

Serves: 6

Cleverly piquant with a balanced taste.

Ingredients:

30	each	Shrimp, under seven to the pound, peel and deveined, tail-on
1/3	recipe	Yucatan spice rub
1	cup	Southwestern crust, see recipe on page 85
1/2	cup	Olive oil, extra-virgin
12	oz.	Anaheim-vanilla syrup, see recipe page 95
3	cups	Wheatberry rice, see recipe page 181
1	bunch	Mint sprigs, garni

Instructions:

After cleaning shrimp dip into the rub, pat into the southwestern crust. Saute quickly in very hot olive oil. Drain well.

SAUCE: Just make the glaze and spread at bottom of plate and lay the shrimp atop when done.

SALAD: Cook the wheatberry recipe to make three cups. Mix with a little of the syrup listed above. Toss lightly and using a triangle mold, fill with 1/2 cup of the rice and pack tight. Overturn onto the center of the plate.

Place the shrimp surrounding the rice.

GARNISH: Use sprigs of mint leaf.

Grilled rack of shrimp

Serve: 6

Can be served cold as an appetizer.

Ingredients:

36	each	Shrimp, extra large, de-vein and butterfly
2	tbs.	Creole cajun seasonings, see recipes on page 83
2	oz.	Herb oil, see recipe below
4	tbs.	Peach-orange coulis, see recipe on page 108
6	each	Rosemary stalks, peel and sharpen the ends

Instructions:

De-vein the shrimp and cut down the backs to butterfly open. Lay out flat. Mix 1/2 cajun spice with the oil. Thread the shrimp onto the rosemary skewers. Marinate the shrimp (in the refrigerator) for 1 day in the oil mixture.

Take the shrimp out and shake off the excess oil. Lay flat and add the other half of the seasoning mix. Pat onto the shrimp lightly. Heat grill coals to grey. Oil the slats of the grill and place the skewers over the coals making sure that the rosemary herb end isn't over the flame. Cook then flip over and finish quickly. When finished, cool.

Place on service plate and drizzle with the peach coulis.

Herb oil

1 cup

Ingredients:

1	tbs.	Fresh basil, chopped finely
1	teas.	Fresh thyme, finely chopped
1/2	teas.	Rosemary, finely chopped
1	tbs.	Chervil, finely chopped
2	tbs.	Shallots, finely chopped
1	tbs.	Garlic, crushed and finely chopped
1/2	cup	Extra-virgin olive oil
1/4	cup	Canola oil

Instructions:

In a bowl, mix everything together and cover. Let ingredients macerate overnight before using as a marinade on any foods.

Herbena Stripe Bass

Serves: 4

A locally raised fish that takes well to herbed preparations.

Ingredients:

2	each	Stripe bass, about two lbs. each
As needed		Oil
4	oz.	Herbena chimi-churri, see recipe on page 83
6	oz.	Exotic fruit sauce, see recipe on page 102

Instructions:

Make the chimi-churri, see recipe on page 83. Lay the fillets of stripe bass in the chimi-churri for two hours. Remove and wipe off excess. Next make the sauce, see recipe and save until needed. Lightly oil the surface of the wok with a paper towel dampened with oil. Quickly sear the fillets in a hot wok. Caramelize the exterior of the fillets and place in a 350 degree oven for three minutes to finish cooking. Remove to a platter and keep warm.

Next nappe the serving plates in an artful fashion with the sauce. Lay the finished filets over the sauce.

Macadamia Stripe Bass

Serves: 6

Ingredients:

2	lbs.	Stripe bass fillet, five oz. each
As needed		Salt & pepper, 5:1 ratio
6	tbs.	Orange juice concentrate
9	tbs.	Macadamia nuts, toasted golden
1	each	Lemon, zest
1	each	Lime, zest
2	teas.	"Hot salt", find in Asian markets
16	oz.	Mango beurre blanc, see recipe on page 105
1	recipe	Coconut rice, see recipe on page 167

Hints:

This example of the "Fun and Playful" food combinations used in South Florida will surely be a hit on your table.

Instructions:

Season fillets and brush each with one tbs. of orange juice concentrate. Let marinate 1/2 hour. Top with a mixture of the dry ingredients - ground fine. Place on baking sheet and bake quickly in a 400 degree oven for five minutes. Let topping brown. Place the rice in a pyramid mold, pack firmly and then overturn onto the plate. Lay the fillet slightly off to one side of the rice. Nappe the plate with the mango beurre blanc.

Pepper-spiked Mako Shark

Serves: 6

INGREDIENTS:

3	LBS.	Mako, cut into 6 steaks
3	CUPS	Sauce exotica, see recipe on page 102
6	TBS.	Cracked black pepper
5	KERNEL	Garlic, roasted, smashed (see note below)
6	CUPS	Cous cous, see recipe on page 169
24	PIECES	Asparagus stalks, trimmed and blanched (see below)
4	OZ.	Opal basil vinaigrette, see recipe on page 73

INSTRUCTIONS:

For Fish.... Heat a wok or a cast iron skillet super-hot. Pat the steaks dry and then rub with the roasted garlic (see notes below). Then press the cracked black pepper into the mako steaks. Sear both sides of the steaks quickly in pan. It only takes seconds. Lift out and place on a roasting pan and finish cooking in a 350 degree oven for seven minutes per inch of steak thickness. Take out of the oven and place in center of the plate.

For sauce.... Make recipe in book and nappe the plate after the mako steaks are in place.

For Cous Cous.... Make recipe on page 169 and place in a stainless steel pyramid. Invert on plate at the 12:00 setting.

For Asparagus... Use small spears and blanch in boiling water for two minutes. Remove and shock quickly in a ice water bath. Warm asparagus in the opal-basil vinaigrette right before serving. Place onto the plate at the 10:00 and 2:00.

P.S.
Instead of regular green asparagus, use the purple variety that is available from California starting the first week of April. To blanch the asparagus, cook in a microwave, in a covered container, for 1 minute or until slightly tender. Shock in ice water bath - so they keep their color - and warm as you do for the green asparagus.

Cooking hints....

To roast the garlic... Just place a well oiled head of garlic into a 325 degree oven and cook until it becomes as soft as an overripe melon.

Cracked black pepper.... Use the fresh Puerto Rican variety.

Yucatan seared Swordfish

Serves: 4

Ingredients:

4	6 oz.	Swordfish loin, steaks
4	oz.	Yucatan rub, see recipe on page 89
1	cup	Red curry-grapefruit sauce, see recipe on page 101
As needed		Oil
As needed		Citrus sections, as needed

Instructions:
Make the rub according to the recipe's directions. Clean the swordfish loin of all discolorations. Rub the entire loin with the rub and refrigerate two days. Take out, brush off the marinade. Cut into steaks. Make the sauce according to the recipe. Heat a wok or a heavy cast iron skillet until hot. Rub the pan with paper towel dampened with a little oil. Sear the pieces of swordfish quickly.

Remove from pan and finish cooking in a preheated 400 degree oven for seven minutes per inch of steak size of thickness. Remove from oven and let rest on a warm platter so juices will run onto the platter and not your presentation plate. Take the sauce and nappe the plate, lay the steak atop the sauce.

Hints:

Swordfish is always cut into loin steaks. The quick searing action in the skillet produces an intriguing flavor combination. For this combination of flavors, Beaujolais Nouveau makes an interesting "Taste-Variance" for this dish

Swordfish with Asian pear and Tarragon bud "Coulis-grette"

Serves: 6

Ingredients:

As needed		Salt and pepper, 5:1 ratio
3	lbs.	Swordfish steaks, 7-8 oz. cuts
1/2	cup	Tarragon buds
6	oz.	Tarragon vinegar
1 1/2	each	Asian pears (save half pears)
6	oz.	Olive oil
2	each	Egg yolks
2	cups	Gourmet baby lettuces
6	each	Yellow plum tomatoes, split

Instructions:

Season swordfish steaks. Oil the slats of the grill. Cook steaks about 10 minutes per inch of thickness. While they are cooking make the "coulisgrette"....

To make the "coulis-grette", place the chopped Asian pear (save half of the pear for garnishes later), tarragon buds, and vinegar in a cuisinart. Blend well. Add the oil slowly. Add the egg yolks and let run to thicken. Season with a little salt and pepper.

Place the steak on the plate, scatter the other half of the Asian pear around the plate with a few well placed yellow tomatoes. Make a small salad bundle at the top of the plate. Nappe the entire presentation with the pear "coulisgrette".

Hints:

Used in this way, a complex crescendo of flavors punctuate this recipe highlighting the best of both sauce ingredients.

SESAME SEARED TUNA LOIN

SERVES: 4

CAN ALSO BE COOKED ON A GRILL. TRY PAIRING THIS DISH WITH A LIGHT CHIANTI WINE.

INGREDIENTS:

1 1/2	LBS.	TUNA LOIN, CUT INTO 16 TRIANGLES
2	TBS.	SESAME OIL
1	CUP	SESAME SEEDS, BLACK AND WHITE MIXED
1	CUP	UGLIFRUIT COULISGRETTE, SEE RECIPE ON PAGE 74
1 1/2	CUPS	BASMATI RICE, PRECOOKED

INSTRUCTIONS:

CUT THE TUNA LOIN INTO EQUAL PORTIONS. MARINATE TUNA FOR UP TO THREE HOURS IN THE SESAME OIL. DRY AND COAT IN THE SESAME SEEDS, SLIGHTLY PATTING THEM INTO THE FLESH. HEAT THE WOK AND FILL WITH SOME SESAME OIL FROM THE MARINADE.

PLACE THE STEAKS IN WOK AND SEAR QUICKLY. TURN TO GET ALL THE EDGES LIGHTLY BROWNED. NAPPE THE PLATE AND THEN PLACE A SCOOP OF RICE IN THE CENTER OF THE PLATE. SLICE AND SHINGLE TUNA AND PLACE ALONG SIDE THE RICE ATOP THE SAUCE. SEE PAGE 132.

WAHOO, THE FISHERMAN'S FISH

SERVES: 10

THIS COMBINATION OF FISH AND SAUCE IS NOT EXCLUSIVE TO PAPAYA B.B.Q., IT CAN BE PAIRED WITH MANY OF THE SAUCES AVAILABLE IN THIS BOOK.

INGREDIENTS:

4-5	LBS.	WAHOO FILLETS, SEVEN OZ. EACH
1/4	CUP	WAHOO MARINADE, SEE RECIPE ON PAGE 84
4	CUP	FRESH FRUIT SALSA, SEE RECIPE 50
1	PT.	PAPAYA B.B.Q. SAUCE, SEE RECIPE 107

INSTRUCTIONS:

TRIM THE FILLETS. CUT PORTIONS ABOUT SEVEN OZ. MARINATE IN THE WAHOO MARINADE FOR ABOUT 30 MINUTES. MAKE THE SALSA AND LET MACERATE WHILE PREPARING THE FISH. PREPARE THE SAUCE AND USE FOR NAPPE-ING THE PLATE IN A HAPHAZARD FASHION. PLACE THE FISH IN A WOK TO SEAR QUICKLY. FINISH IN A 375 DEGREE OVEN FOR ABOUT 10 MINUTES, DEPENDING ON THICKNESS OF FILLET.

PLACE THE COOKED FILLET ATOP THE NAPPED PLATE ABUTTING AGAINST THE SALSA.

Simply Yellowtail

Serves: 6

Ingredients:
6	EACH	Yellowtail fillets, about five oz. each
18	OZ.	Passionfruit "coulisgrette", see recipe 74

Instructions:
Heat coals to gray. While you are heating coals, marinate the fillets in half the coulisgrette. Grill after marinating about 30 minutes - over lightly oiled slats -- cook until flaky. Carefully remove to a platter and keep warm.

When you are ready to serve, nappe the platter and fish with the other half of the coulisgrette.

Plantain crusted Yellowtail

Serves: 4

Ingredients:
4	EACH	Yellowtail snapper, 6 oz. each
As needed		Salt and pepper, 5:1 ratio
1	EACH	Key lime, juiced
2	OZ.	Orange juice concentrate
1	EACH	Plantain, green, sliced very thinly
1/4	CUP	Japanese bread crumbs
Dash		Chipotle pepper, dry, crushed

Instructions:

Prepare the fillets...
Season and flavor with the lime juice. Paint with the half frozen orange juice concentrate. Coat with crust (see next note). Bake for about seven minutes at 350 degrees.

Crust...
Slice the plantains and deep fry until golden. Drain, cool and then crush in a Cuisinart. Add the bread crumbs, chipotle and salt. Crush very fine. Sprinkle over top the fillets.

Hints:
I use yellowtail straight out of Key West for this recipe. Being fresh and consistent in quality, Yellowtail is one of South Florida's favorite seafood entree choices. This recipe could be used with any delicately flavored fish. Accompany with a mango salsa or puree.

Feathers and Bones

Cattle can not be raised in the Island Nations of the Caribbean~ due to the heat and in some cases the terrain.

Adobo Poulet

Serves: 4

The simplicity of these ingredients will build a complex arrangement of taste.

Ingredients:
3	each	Garlic, crushed
1	each	Shallot, fine
1/2	teas.	Cumin, toasted, grind fine
1	each	Bay leaf, crushed
1/2	teas.	Oregano
1/2	teas.	Thyme
1	tbs.	Cilantro
3	tbs.	Sour orange juice
2	tbs.	Annatto infused oil (see side bar)
As needed		Salt & pepper
2	each	Double poultry breast (12 oz.)
12	oz.	Orange peach coulis, page 108

Instructions:
Saute garlic and shallot, add the next seven ingredients. When softpuree in blender to emulsify completely. Cool. Coat the breasts with this marinade and let sit for 30 minutes.

Grill over hot coals. Brush with more of the marinade while cooking. Watch for flare-ups. Cook breasts about 12 minutes turning often. Nappe sauce on the plate and set the breast atop the sauce.

Cut each breast separately, place on plate with the passionate rice, see recipe on page 172.

.

The lipstick tree, as it is known in South America, was used for facial decorations by the ancient Incans-hence the name.

Annatto Oil

Serves: 10

Ingredients:
1 Tbs. Annatto seeds, from the Lipstick (annatto) tree (See bottom of page)
1 cup Olive oil, extra-virgin

Instructions:
Heat oil slowly for three four minutes. Add the seeds and let stew for 5 minutes. Strain and refrigerate until needed.

ANAHEIM CHICKEN

SERVES: 8

INGREDIENTS:

4	EACH	CHICKEN BREAST, DOUBLE LOBE
AS NEEDED		SALT AND PEPPER, 5:1 RATIO
4	OZ.	ANAHEIM-VANILLA SYRUP, SEE RECIPE PAGE 95
2	RECIPES	YUCCA DUMPLINGS, SEE RECIPE PAGE 182
1 1/2	CUPS	MAMEY SALSA, SEE RECIPE IN SIDE NOTE

INSTRUCTIONS:

SEASON BREASTS. OIL THE GRILL AFTER THE COALS ARE TURNED TO GRAY. LAY THE CHICKEN BREASTS ON THE SLATS AND COOK 12 MINUTES, TURNING MANY TIMES. BASTE WITH ANAHEIM-VANILLA GLAZE. WHEN DONE, SLICE THE CHICKEN BREAST ON A SEVER BIAS. PLACE ATOP THE DUMPLINGS AND THEN DRIZZLE WITH THE SAUCE. SPOON SALSA OVER EVERYTHING, SCATTERING DECORATIVELY AROUND THE PLATE.

SALSA

MAMEY IS A FRUIT THAT WILL REMIND YOU OF EATING A PEACH WITH A DISTINCTIVE HONEY AND MOLASSES SWEETNESS, THAT IS LIGHTLY DUSTED WITH A TOUCH OF NUTMEG. USE THE BASIC SALSA RECIPE **ON PAGE 50** AND JUST SUBSTITUTE THE MAMEY IN EQUAL PROPORTIONS AS THE FRUIT IN THE RECIPE. THIS GOES JUST AS WELL WITH DUCK.

CARIBBEAN-LATIN CHICKEN

SERVES: 8

INGREDIENTS:

1	CUP	MANGO SEVILLE ORANGE COULIS, SEE RECIPE ON PAGE 73
1/4	CUP	CARIBBEAN OIL
1 1/2	OZ.	"JERK", YOUR RECIPE
1/4	CUP	SHALLOTS, FINELY CHOPPED.
1/4	CUP	CILANTRO STEMS, CHOPPED
1	STALKS	LEMONGRASS, CHOPPED
1 1/2	PTS.	YUCATAN SPICE, SEE RECIPE PAGE 89
8	EACH	CHICKEN BREAST, SKINLESS, 6-8 OZ. EACH
1	CUP	SALSA-MAMEY, SEE SIDEBAR NOTES

INSTRUCTIONS:

MIX FIRST SEVEN INGREDIENTS IN CUISINART AND THEN COAT THE CHICKEN BREAST. LET MARINATE OVER NIGHT. GRILL OVER HOT-GRAY COALS. COOK ABOUT 12 MINUTES TURNING MANY TIMES. BASTE WITH THE MARINADE AS IT COOKS. PLACE ON THE PLATE WITH THE SALSA AS A GARNISH AND SAUCE SUBSTITUTE.

Chicken with Fire-roasted onions

Serves: 4

Ingredients:

2	each	Chicken breast, split, 6 oz. each
2	oz.	Molasses
1	teas.	Balsamic vinegar
1	teas.	Rhum (*the old Pirate spelling of "Rum"*)
As needed		Salt and pepper, 5:1 ratio
1	each	Red onion, sliced 1/4 inch thick
2	each	Scallions, bias cut
3	oz.	Shallots, finely chopped
4	oz.	Guava scented B.B.Q sauce, see recipe on page 103
As needed		Sun-nature rice, see recipe on page 178

Instructions:

Mix the molasses with the next four ingredients. Marinate the breast for two hours. Heat grill and oil slats. When the coals are grey, cook the marinated breasts. About six minutes on one side, four minutes on the other and then again three minutes more on the first side.

As they are cooking, quickly roast the sliced onions over the flame. Saute the other scallions and shallots and toss all the onions together with half the B.B.Q sauce. Place in a mound in the center of each plate. Add rice to plate. After the breast has a chance to rest (for five minutes after cooking), slice on a bias and lay around the onion mixture. Drizzle the other half of the B.B.Q. sauce around the plate.

Grilling

The ingredients in this recipe are mixed in the manner that enhances the grilling effect on the chicken breast.

The natural caramelization effect of the grill enhances the tastes of the onions. Both the chicken and the onions work really well together.

Grilled Chicken and Peach Coulis

Serves: 15

This is an excellent recipe to pair with berry rice recipe page 181. If you want a recipe to take with you to your next outside event, this is the one.

Ingredients:

15	each	Single chicken breast
1	recipe	Yin and Yang recipe on page 89
As needed		Olive oil
1/2	cup	Shallots, chopped finely
1/2	cup	Rice wine vinegar
3	each	Bay leaf, bruised
1	tbs.	Green peppercorns
1	qt.	Peach puree
1/2	cup	White wine
As needed		Whole butter, soft

Instructions:

Make the Yin and Yang marinade, see instructions on page 89. Marinate chicken for three hours in the marinade before grilling. Heat coals to grey stage. Brush grill with a little oil. Cook breast over coals until done, baste with marinade occasionally while it cooks.

To make sauce:

Sweat shallots with a little oil. Deglaze with vinegar and wine. Add the seasonings, and the puree. Let cook until slightly thickened. Whip in the butter over a low flame. Don't boil.

Serve the chicken breast over top the red onion jam (see side bar) and nappe the sauce over the chicken.

Tips:

To make peach puree, peel overripe peaches and puree with a food ricer. You need a thick puree.

Red Onion Jam

2 oz. Olive oil
2 each Red onions, sliced thin
As needed salt and pepper
3 oz. Rum
4 oz. Sugarcane juice
2 oz. Red wine
1/2 teas. Allspice
1/3 teas. Mace

Directions:

Saute the onions, season and cook until translucent. Add the liquids and the rest of the seasonings. Cook down until very limp and reduce liquids to a syrupy consistency.

Lacquered Duck

Serves: 2

Ingredients:

2	stalks	Ginger, rough cut
6	stalks	Lemongrass, rough cut
4	each	Limes, halved
8	oz.	Honey
As needed		Water
1	each	Long-Island duckling
1/2	cup	Honey, orange blossom
4	oz.	Lemongrass and Soursop sauce, see recipe on page 105

Instructions:

Place duck in a pot large enough to hold it and fill to cover with water. Add the lemongrass, lime, honey and ginger. Boil for 20 minutes. Poke the duck's skin with a sharp fork as it cooks so the fat just under the skin leaches out.

In the meantime, place the honey in a teflon pan over a very hot flame. Boil rapidly until the honey caramelizes. Pour in the lemongrass and soursop sauce, off the heat.

When the ducks is finished, cool slightly and brush with the honey mixture. Let air dry slightly then brush again. Place in the refrigerator uncovered to dry and crisp the skin.

Oven roast in a 300 degree oven for 1 1/4 hours. The skin will turn a deep brown and will crisp as it cooks. The skin should be at crackling perfection when done.

Ducks

For this recipe you want to use a 5 pound duck.

The use of limes is very important for the crisp-factor of the duck

If you find that the skin is not to your liking, try broiling under the element of the oven for 3 minutes until the skin really crisps up.

Full Moon Party in the Caribbean

Citrus-Coffee Marinated Moulade Duck Breast

Serves: 4

Ingredients:

2	each	Moulade duck breast, 1 1/2 lbs.
2	tbs.	Jamaican Blue Mountain coffee
2	oz.	Teriakyi sauce
1	cup	Orange juice
1/4	cup	Orange zest, finely chopped
1/4	cup	Grapefruit juice
6	each	Peppercorns, white, crushed
2	oz.	Sesame oil
1/12	cup	Sprouted mustard seed sauce, see page 106

Hints:

Use the recipe with the black-eyed pea compote found on page 165 for both the veggie and starch. The black-eyed peas are typically a southern dish, yet I think work great in this recipe.

Instructions:

Mix all the ingredients but the breast and the mustard seed sauce. Place the breast into the marinade and let rest in the refrigerator for up to three hours. Remove from marinade and place over gray coals of an oiled grill. Cook the fat side down first on the highest setting for the rack. Let cook till skin is slightly crisp. Watch for flame flare-ups.

As the breasts cooks, the meat will start to sweat on the upper side. Lower rack, turn the breast over and quickly grill over the high heat (about 5 minutes) until they are medium rare-125 degrees.

Remove and let rest on a warm platter. Slice across the breast on a bias. Lay aside the starch or veggie accompaniments. Glaze with the sauce.

Green Tea marinated Duck

Serves: 8

Ingredients:

4	each	Long Island duck
1	cup	Ginger, chopped fine
3	tbs.	Orange zest, finely chopped
8	packages	Green tea
2	tbs.	Honey, orange blossom
As needed		Kosher salt
1/2	cup	Orange juice concentrate

Instructions:
Using a sharp knife, cut the skin of the duck in a cross hatched pattern. Mix the spices, flavorings and tea together. Add the juice of the oranges. Sweat in a saute pan. Sweeten with the honey. Cool. Rub all of this into the ducks, and let it marinate in the refrigerator overnight uncovered. This dries out the skin to helps to crisp the skin when cooked. Bake at very slow (at 290 degrees) for 1-1/4 hours. Baste with more orange juice concentrate and pan drippings. Cook until golden brown.

Hints:

I use infused tea marinades for numerous grilled meat dishes. The tea flavor magnifies the roasting effect.

This will go well with a fig and port wine puree (see recipe on page 156).
Flavors don't meld, but bounce off each other creating an explosion of flavors for the senses.

Mango Pork Tenderloin

Serves: 4

Ingredients:

1	EACH	Pork tenderloin, trimmed well
1	CUP	Sugar cane juice, reduced to 2 oz.
1/2	EACH	Orange, zest
2	PINCH	Salt & pepper
6	OZ.	Mango vinegar
2	EACH	Smoked jalapeno, crushed
2	TBS.	Olive oil, extra-virgin
3	EACH	Sage leaves, bruised

Instructions:

Season the cleaned tenderloin with the salt and pepper. Add the zest. Pat into pork. Heat the jalapenos (chipotle chilies) in a 350 degree oven until the skins are crispy brown. Cool and grind into a powder in a coffee grinder.

Meanwhile, reduce the sugarcane juice to a syrup- about two oz. by using a very hot pan. Then mix in vinegar. Reduce again to thicken. Cool. Off the heat, add oil and the rest of the ingredients with the previously roasted and ground jalapenos, making a glaze. Marinate the tenderloin in this at least three hours. Turn half way through the time to make sure the marinade coats all the tenderloin.

Grill the tenderloin over high heat to caramelize the outside to a temperature of 125 degrees. Move to the slower part of the fire, close the lid of the grill and let it cook the rest of the way to an internal temperature of 140 degrees. Remove from grill and let rest a few minutes before slicing.

You can use this marinade for fish and poultry using cilantro in place of sage. You can also substitute passionfruit for the mango vinegar for another great taste.

Hints:

Serve with sprouted mustard seed sauce on page 106.

The reduced sugarcane syrup acts as a marinade and also a grilling accelerator.

The citrus and the smoked jalapenos give depth to the grilling effect.

Pecan smoked Pork loin

Serves: 6

Ingredients:

3	LBS.	Porkloin, boneless
1/4	CUP	Citrus zest, orange, lemon, lime, 2 times as much orange as lemon or lime
1/2	CUP	Yin and Yang marinade, see recipe on page 89
2	BUNCH	Sage, chopped
4	SPRIGS	Rosemary, chopped
10	SPRIGS	Thyme, chopped
1	TBS.	Kosher salt
1/2	PINT	Mulberries
1/2	CUP	Opal basil vinaigrette, see recipe on page 73

Instructions:

Have your butcher trim and tie the loin so it holds its shape while cooking. Marinate the loin in the Yin and Yang marinade for at least three hours. Drain the loin and place on a plate. Dust with zests, herbs and salt. Heat the coals to the grey point. Place the meat in a grill/smoker. Toss the pecan shells on the coals and close the lid. Cook the loin until and internal temperature of 135 degrees is reached-it will take about half an hour. You don't have to overcook pork anymore to make it safe to eat.

Let rest on a warm platter for 10 minutes then slice as needed for each plate.

Vinaigrette....
Mix the opal basil vinaigrette with the mulberries using an immersion hand mixer, until completely blended.

Pecans:

In northern Florida- along the Suwannee river-Pecan trees grow in abundance.

Pecan pie, a staple in north Florida, is a menu highlight in almost every restaurant. When the chefs finished cracking the shells and removing the nut he was left with the empty shells.

What to do with all the extra shells? Soak them in water for at least 30 minutes and toss them on the coals to smoke meats!!

South Florida Po-Poo Platter

Serves: 4

Ingredients:

1	lb.	Alligator ribs
4	each	Quail, de-boned
4	each	Frog legs
2	each	Rabbit loin
1 1/2	cup	Po-poo sauce, see recipe on page 109
2	cup	Green papaya kimchee, see recipe on page 60

Instructions:

Using a half cup of po-poo sauce, (Thin the dipping sauce with water before using as a marinade) marinate ribs and the rabbit loin a day in advance. Roast the alligator ribs slowly at 300 degrees in the oven until fork tender (this can take up to 1 1/2 hours). Grill the quail and rabbit loins over the grey coals of the grill.

When the ribs are finished, glaze with sauce atop the grill. Finish cooking frog legs last.

Plate kimchee in center plate, surround with finished grilled items.

*** Baste all items several times during grilling.

There are several accompanying sides dish recipes that would go well here...

PLANTAINS,

COCONUT RICE,

POTATO PLANKS

Hints:

An occupation that people would think of as exciting would be one that uses an airboat bashing through the water at 35 miles per hour at night. Frog legs are caught by these nocturnal airboat anglers throughout the Everglades.

Spicy Guava B.B.Q Ribs

Serves: 4

Ingredients:

1/2	teas.	Liquid smoke
1/3	cup	Soy sauce
1/4	cup	Molasses
As Needed		Salt and pepper
2	lb.	Baby back pork ribs
1 1/2	cup	Spicy guava glaze, see recipe on page 103

Instructions:

Marinate the ribs in a mixture of the first four ingredients. Let marinate overnight. Remove from the marinade. Season with additional salt and pepper. Grill over gray coals on the upper rack of a covered grill for 1 1/2 hours.

Half way thorough cooking, baste with the sauce repeating every five minutes.

Save a little the of sauce for dipping later.

Hints:

This is a great recipe to pair with a Pinot Noir. The ribs can be cooked in a slow oven (325 degrees) for 2 hours, basting with sauce every half hour. Grill over gray coals to caramelize sauce. Baste with additional sauce. For something really different, try wild boar or alligator ribs. Cook until tender as above.

Tamarind Pork loin with Dovyalis

Serves: 4

This recipe will make you glad you have tastebuds.

Ingredients:

24	oz.	Pork loin
2	oz.	Jerk seasoning, Boston's
1/4	cup	Tamarind pulp
30	each	Dovyalis
As needed		Salt
2	each	Lime juice
1/3	cup	Chicken demi-glace
2	tbs.	Honey, orange blossom
1/8	teas.	Vanilla, see recipe page 112
Pinch		Red pepper flakes
As needed		Frying oil
2	each	Plantains, cut lengthwise
As needed		Salt and pepper, 5:1 ratio
1	each	Starfruit, sliced

Hints:

Dovyalis, the Florida Apricot.

Dovyalis grows sparingly in South Florida, but those of us that have the opportunity, stock up on this fruit when they ripen.

Instructions:

Mix the jerk seasoning with the tamarind pulp. Marinate the pork in it for up two days. The longer, the stronger the flavor will be.

To make the sauce: Peel the dovyalis and place in Cuisinart with the lime juice. Pulse, remove to sauce pan and heat gently. Add the chicken demi and let simmer slowly for flavors to meld. Strain through a fine mesh strainer (a Chinose).

While this is simmering slice the plantains lengthwise tip to tip. Then halve the slices lengthwise again for narrow strips. Deep fry. Cut the starfruit horizontally to form stars. Fire roast the pork for about 35-40 minutes depending on your grill. Check internal temperature for 140 degrees, no more.

Ladle sauce at 6:00 on your plate, lay sliced pork over top of the sauce in a shingled fashion. Place the plantain strips crisscross over entire presentation. Garnish with some starfruit slices.

Use regular apricots if you can't find the Florida apricots.

Fire-roasted Turkey loin

Serves: 8

Ingredients:
- 2 each — Turkey tenderloin
- 2 tbs. — Pommery mustard
- 1 tbs. — Balsamic vinegar
- 1/2 pint — Raspberries
- 1/2 pint — Mulberries, washed well
- 1/3 cup — Opal-basil vinaigrette, see recipe on page 73

Hints:
Mulberries grow wild in Central Florida.

Instructions:
Make the marinade first. Mix the opal-basil vinaigrette with all the rest of the ingredients except the turkey.

To use....
Marinate the tenderloins in half the vinaigrette for at least one hour. Heat coals on the grill until grey. Remove the tenderloins from the marinade, saving what is left over for basting as it cooks. Cook the tenderloins over the lower heat part of the grill. Baste with the leftover marinade every few minutes being careful not to cause flare ups. Remove after 30 minutes and place on platter to rest before cutting. Slice on the bias and shingle layer on the plate.

Pair with a nice mesclun of baby greens salad. Drizzle the plate with the rest of the dressing.

Serve warm or chilled paired with a berry fruit compote for a tasty lunch.

Roasted rack Veal chop

Serves: 4

Ingredients:

4	12 oz.	Veal loin chops
1/2	cup	Opal-basil vinaigrette, see recipe on page 73
2 1/2	cups	Fig puree, see side bar
1	cup	Sprouted mustard seed sauce see recipe on page 106
40	pieces	Haricot verts, blanched
1	tbs.	Butter
As needed		Red bell pepper, small dice
As needed		Cilantro leaves, garnish

Instructions:

Marinate the chops in the opal-basil vinaigrette over night. Heat the coals of the grill until grey. Cook the chops to your liking. Before hand, make the fig puree (follow recipe in the side bar) and cook the haricot verts (tiny french baby string beans) in salted water. Then shock by dipping into a ice water bath to set the color. Warm when needed in a little olive oil when you finish the plate later. Make the mustard seed sauce.

Pipe out the fig puree into rosettes onto plate at 10:00 and 2:00 towards the top of the plate.

Place the beans at 12:00 on plate. Garnish the plate with some tiny diced red bell pepper.

Place the cooked chop in the center of the plate aiming the bone towards the top left quadrant of the plate. Nappe the plates with the sauce.

Garnish with a sprinkling of cilantro leaves.

Fig Puree

Ingredients:
8 oz. Dried figs
1/2 cup Port wine
2 tbs. Shallots, chopped
As needed - Salt and pepper, 5:1 ratio

Instructions:

Soak figs in the wine for at least 3 hours. Add all of this along with the shallots to a saucepan. Heat slowly and let the liquid absorb into the fruit. Add all of this to a cuisinart and pulse the mixture until all is pureed. Season lightly with salt and pepper. Place in a pastry bag fitted with a star tip. Pipe out onto the plate into rosettes.

Where would the "Magic City"

...be without beans and rice.

Veggies

Starchy things

Fusion Noodles—see page 180, with a Seabass with spicy glazed mangos—on page 49

Caribbean Lobster and Soursop

STARCHES
What is a starch, how is it used and, how does cooking effect it?

Plants produce starches.....

Water, sunlight, carbon dioxide and the photosynthesis process within plants produce starch molecules. When these molecules form long chains (called Amylose) and short chains (Amylopectin) they build upon each other to construct plant cells.

We use starches to thicken liquids in cookery. They thicken by absorbing the liquid in which they are added. As the liquid heats, the starch swells and then bursts, absorbing the liquid that it has been added to. By slowing down a sauce's movement, the starch molecules cluster with each other and form layers of a thickened mass. The less free liquid there is, the thicker a sauce becomes. Holding up to forty times their weight, starches are used according to the clarity in a sauce.

If you don't mind a cloudy finished product, like puddings, use the long chain starches. Amylose (long-chain) starches are made from the flours of corn and wheat. Amylopectin (short-chain) starches like Arrowroot, will produce a clear finished product.

Affects on how starches thicken.
> Sugar, acids and egg yolks all counteract the starch's ability to thicken. Sugar deprives water from the starch, which they need to expand and then burst. Acids (vinegars, lemon juice, etc....) can cause the starch granules to disintegrate too soon. Egg yolk enzymes can eventually destroy starch cells.

Simple hints how to use the starches.....
> Don't ever use raw pineapple in a sauce that needs to be thickened.
> Completely mix the dry starches into a liquid medium: water, butter, etc...
> Make sure your sauce is boiling before you add the slurry AND it has come to a boil again before you add additional thickening.

How can you tell when a starch has reached its total capacity to thicken?
> Usually the sauce becomes clear (in the case of Amylopectins-cornstarch) after the last addition of the starch. Temperature is a good guide on its limits to thicken. If the sauce temperature is 150 to 160 degrees, it is very close to the thickest it can be.

GRAIN COOKERY

ITEM	****GRAIN to liquid (cups)	FINAL YIELD	COOK TIME
Barley	1: 2	4	45 Minutes.
Kasha	1: 2	2	20 Minutes.
Cous cous	1: 1.2	2	20 minutes.
Grits	1: 3.5-4	3	25 minutes.
Millet	1: 2	3	35 minutes.
Polenta	1: 3.5	3	45 minutes.
Risotto	1: 2.5-3	3	30 minutes.
Basmati	1: 1.5	3	25 minutes.
Rice	1: 1.5	4	30 minutes.
Wild rice	1: 3	4	45 minutes.
Brown rice	1: 3	4	40 minutes.
Cracked wheat	1: 2	3	20 minutes.

****Ratios of grain to liquid (or stock) are always flexible according to type of grain and how old it is.

Peoples from around the equatorial regions of the world never used wheat flour before the onslaught of the Western cultures. Before the influence of this western civilization, the "Eastern" world never knew wheat. Only cultures from the northern European latitudes have histories of wheat flour usage.

Grains are....

the single best source of fiber and starch for a "Spa" cuisine style of diet. Buy and use only the freshest of products. First toast the grains in a hot skillet before you use them. Afterwards cook in flavorful stocks.

Cous cous is not a grain (but a pasta) however, is used in the same fashion as other grains.
Quinoa, an ancient grain discovered by the Incan race, has a caviar texture and bite.
Rye grows wherever wheat grows. It lacks gluten and has a grassy flavor.
Fake grains like; "Wild Rice", are a grass seed and not a grain.

The grain with the greatest efficiency of land usage is rice. It lacks some of the nutrient values of wheat, but makes up for this with uncommon versatility.

BEANS

After soaking the beans, you should always cook all bean products in flavorful stock. The addition of a standard Mirepoix (of celery, carrots and onions) is a basic necessity.

BEANS:	SOAKING TIME:	COOKING TIME:
Black	4 hrs.	1 hour
Black-eyed peas	4 hrs.	1.5 hrs.
Chick peas	4 Hrs.	2.5 hrs.
Fava	12 hrs.	3 hrs.
Northern	4 hrs.	1 hour
Kidney	4 hrs.	1 hour
Lentils	2 hrs.	40 minutes.
Lima	4 hrs.	1.5 hrs.
Navy	4 hrs.	2 hrs.
Split peas	2 hrs.	30 minutes.
Pigeon peas	2 hrs.	45 minutes
Soybeans	4 hrs.	1.5 hrs.
Appaloosa	4 hrs.	2 hrs.

SWORDFISH WITH CORN AND
BLACK BEAN SALAD ON PAGE 165

VIEW FROM MY HOME
ON TORTOLA

Macrobotic Azuki Beans

Serves: 10

Ingredients:

1	lb.	Azuki beans
1	qt.	Passionfruit juice
1	each	Bay leaf
1	lb.	Onions, caramelized
1	oz.	Key lime juice
2	oz.	Pickled ginger, finely diced
2	each	Scallions, sliced
1	each	Scotch bonnet pepper
1/2	each	Red bell pepper, diced
1/2	each	Yellow bell pepper, diced
10	stems	Cilantro leaves, chopped
1	each	Starfruit, diced
1/2	each	Mango, diced

Hints:

Azuki Beans are found in Asian Markets.

Add no salt or additional spices. This is a macrobiotic natural combination of ingredients.

Directions:

Soak the beans overnight to quicken their cooking. Cook the beans in the passionfruit juice and the next three ingredients, stirring constantly. Add water as necessary as the liquid is absorbed~until the beans are tender. It will be about 20 minutes.

Meanwhile, cut all the veggies about the same size as the beans, except for the scotch bonnet peppers. Cut them very finely. In the last five minutes of cooking, add the rest of the ingredients. Let simmer until the veggies are soft and the "stew" is completely cooked. Serve as a starch for seafood dishes.

Black-Eyed Pea Compote

Serves: 4

> **Hints:** Use this with braised dishes that call for stewing the protein in a flavorful stock to finish its cooking.

Ingredients:

1	cup	Black-eyed peas
1/2	cup	Chicken consomme
1	tbs.	Olive oil, extra-virgin
1/3	cup	Ramps, sliced thin
1	cup	Tomato concasse, diced
1	tbs.	Balsamic vinegar
1	tbs.	Cilantro, chopped
As needed		Salt and pepper, 5:1 ratio
1/2	teas.	Thai peanut seasoning blend

Instructions:

Cook the peas in a chicken consomme until done. Drain. Sweat (cook slowly in oil) the ramps in a warm skillet with one tablespoon oil. Toss in the tomatoes. Stir well. Mix in the oil and vinegar. Season with a little salt and pepper and quickly toss in the cilantro. Sprinkle in the Thai peanut seasonings (*You can find the peanut seasoning at most Asian markets*). Toss in the cooked beans and mix well.

Black Bean and Corn Compote

Serves: 6-8 as a salad or 12 appetizers

Cook beans with a dash of sugar. Great veggie for poultry and seafood dishes.

Ingredients:

2	cups	Black beans
1	cup	Corn kernels, cooked
1/4	cup	Cilantro, chopped
2	teas.	Lime juice, freshly squeezed
2	teas.	Olive oil, extra virgin
1	teas.	Guarapo, syrup
1	each	Scallion, sliced on a bias
1/3	each	Red bell pepper, finely diced

Instructions:

Cook the black beans in a flavorful chicken stock or consomme. Cool. Toss with all the rest of the ingredients.

Baby Bliss Potato and Maytag Blue Cheese

Serves: 10 portions

Ingredients:

30	EACH	Small red bliss potatoes
As needed		Salt and white pepper, 5:1 ratio
1	oz.	Onion, fine, sweat
2	teas.	Butter
2	teas.	Pernod
8	oz.	Blue cheese
1	lb.	Goat cheese
1	dash each	Salt and black pepper
1	teas.	Chives, snipped
1/2	teas.	Garlic, crushed
1	teas.	Garlic oil

Instructions:

First step....Slice off the top and bottom end of each baby potato. Place them in a pot that will accommodate all with plenty of surrounding water. Season the water with a lot of salt and white pepper. Cook until a fork can slide in and out of the potato. Remove and then cool. Hollow out the top half of each potato and reserve until filling is ready.

Next...Sweat onion in butter until soft. Add the Pernod liquor. Cool. Then mix all the rest of the ingredients - in a mixer - one at a time. Mix thoroughly so that both cheeses are well incorporated. Place this mixture into a pastry bag and pipe into hollowed, pre-blanched baby bliss potatoes from above.

To Use....Place these stuffed potatoes on a greased baking sheet and place into a 350 degree oven and bake for about 15 minutes. Serve three per person.

Use these potatoes for garnish of beef dishes and as a substructure on which you can place grilled meats and seafood atop to build towering presentations.

Hints:

Maytag is a name brand you should look for when purchasing a Blue cheese. It is creamy and rich and I feel better tasting then many products out there. The combination of blue cheese and steak is a perfect match, so use this with any steak entree.

Chick Pea salad

Serves: 6

Ingredients:

1/4	cup	Olive oil, extra virgin
1/4	cup	Balsamic vinegar
1/2	teas.	Garlic, crushed
1/2	teas.	Salt
16	oz.	Chick peas, cooked
9	oz.	Haricot verts, blanched
1 1/2	cup	Plum tomatoes, diced
1	tbs.	Tarragon buds, chopped

Instructions:

Whip the first four ingredients together. Toss in the chick peas. Toss in the rest of the ingredients and coat with the vinaigrette. Drain slightly before plating.

Hints:

Use in combination with any seafood or poultry dish.

Chick peas are used dry in the Caribbean. Of course you should soak overnight and cook using three times as much water or chicken stock. Use the guide found earlier in this chapter.

Coconut rice

Serves: 4

In the Virgin Islands, this is a common side dish. It goes with roasted pork, curried chicken or any seafood dish.

Ingredients:

1/4	cup	Olive oil, extra virgin
1	teas.	Garlic, crushed
1	each	Onion, chopped well
1	cup	Rice
1/2	teas.	Salt and pepper, 5:1 ratio
1	cup	Coconut milk
1 1/2	cups	Chicken stock
1	tbs.	Thyme

Instructions:

Saute the first three ingredients. Toss rice into the saute and season. Add in the rest of the ingredients (except thyme) and cook on high heat until liquid disappears. Lower heat to a light simmer. Cover the pot with a lid and let cook another 15 minutes, until the rice is completely soft and tender. Fluff with a roasting fork and toss in the thyme.

Homestead Corn Compote

Serves: 8

Ingredients:

6	each	Corn cobs
1	each	Red bell pepper, diced
1	each	Scallions, diced
1/2	each	Cucumber, diced
2	tbs.	Cider vinegar
1/3	teas.	Tabasco sauce
1	tbs.	Dijon mustard
2	tbs.	Cilantro, chopped
2	tbs.	Olive oil

Instructions:
Using fresh corn in the husks, blanch the corn quickly in water. Remove the kernels from the cob. Cut the rest of the veggies the same size as the corn kernels and toss with the corn.

Dressing...Mix the cider vinegar with the rest of the ingredients and pour over the veggies. Marinate a few minutes and serve.

To Use:
This can be heated very quickly if you like in a hot skillet. Us the warm compote as a base or garnish for any entree, spreading it over the bottom of a plate in a decorative way.

Hints:

The corn that comes directly from Homestead, is probably the best in the state. Corn is a true Southerner' dinner ingredient. It is frequently used in the Caribbean in various ways. But using fresh on the cob, is my favorite.

White Bean Compote
Serves: 10

Ingredients:
3	lbs.	White beans, pre-cooked
3/4	lb.	Tomato concasse
4	oz.	Carrots, diced, blanched
4	oz.	Pepper, red bell, diced
2	oz.	Onion, diced
1/3	cup	Tomato paste
1	cup	Chicken demi, see hints
1	teas.	Sugar
1/4	cup	Madeira wine
1/4	cup	Beurre manie

Hints:
Heat the chicken stock and reduce 1 1/2 qts. of stock to one cup forming a demi glace

For the compote use the demi glace as a moisturizer for the beans and finish their cooking.

Instructions:
Toss all veggies in hot oil. Add the stock and bring to simmer. Add just a bit of sugar. Add the tomato paste, let thicken slightly. Add the wine and then the beurre manie (butter that has been first tossed in flour). Let simmer for five minutes so the flavors meld completely.

Spiced Cous Cous
Serves: 8-10

Ingredients:
1	teas.	Olive oil, extra-virgin
1/3	bunch	Scallions, bias cut
2	each	Plum tomatoes, concasse
1 1/4	pts.	Water
1/3	teas.	Cumin, ground
3/4	teas.	Salt
1	teas.	Curry powder
1	each	Cinnamon sticks
1	pt.	Cous cous, brown

Hints:
Sweating veggies is cooking them slowly over a low flame until soft.

Instructions:
Sweat (see hints) first three ingredients over a low flame and save for the rest of the next part of the recipe.

Boil the water with the seasonings and pour over the cous cous. Toss and cover, for about 15 minutes, letting cous cous absorb the water. Remove cover and fork to separate and fluff. Cool slightly and add the veggies. Serve warm.

Cou Cou, Caribbean polenta

Serves: 6-10 *(depending on wether you are serving a side dish or as a dinner portion)*

This is a dish that transcends everything Caribbean, a must have side dish when cooking a traditional Caribbean family feast. You can use this recipe as a filling (stuffing) the belly of a baked whole fish.

Hints:

Fungi another name for Cou Cou is a daily staple for "Country Folk".

Cou Cou doesn't typically call for cream or butter. Most Caribbean peoples cook it vegetarian style.

Like the Italian version, enrichened with cream, this is great with grouper or snapper.

Ingredients:

1	oz.	Olive oil, extra-virgin
4	each	Garlic cloves, crushed
4	oz.	Onions, finely diced
1/3	bunch	Scallions, sliced
8	each	Okras, sliced
2	ears	Corn on the cob, shucked
3	cups	Veggie stock
1/2	cup	Heavy cream
1/3	cup	Cilantro, chopped
3/4	tbs.	Salt and pepper, 5:1 ratio
1	cup	Cormeal

Instructions:
Cook the first three ingredients very, slowly over a low flame. Add the okra and corn. Raise the heat, cook 15 minutes until okra softens. Add the stock and boil. Season and add the cornmeal. Stir rapidly with a wooden spoon as it is cooking. Cook 20 minutes.

The cou-cou will pull away from the pot as it finishes cooking and becomes thickened. Serve warm along with any seafood dish.

Fusion Pasta
Serves: 10

Ingredients:
As needed		Olive oil, extra-virgin
3	tbs.	Shallots, fine
1/2	cup	Calabaza
1/2	cup	Ramps
2	cup	Bok choy tops
1/2	cup	Mango, julienne
10	cup	Penne pasta, blanched
As needed		Olive oil, extra-virgin
1	cup	Sprouted Mustard seed sauce, see recipe on page 106
As needed		Cherry tomatoes, halved

Instructions:
Cut the calabaza and ramps into julienne strips. Blanch the veggies by steaming. Cool. Toss with a little olive oil. Then saute with the shallots. Don't caramelized. Warm the pre-cooked pasta and save warm with a little oil. Toss veggies with the pasta and warm quickly with a little sauce. Garnish with cherry tomatoes.

Hints: For the Bok choy, use the dark green top leaves like you would spinach. Chiffonade cut (that is shred very fine with a knife). The Bok choy will cook a lot better than spinach.

Citrus Noodles
Serves: 4

Ingredients:
1	tbs.	Garlic, crushed
2	tbs.	Olive oil, extra virgin
3	tbs.	Tamari
2	tbs.	Sherry
2	tbs.	Rice wine vinegar
2	tbs.	Sesame oil
1/2	teas.	Chili-garlic paste
1/2	each	Orange peel-grated
1/2	lb.	Fresh chow mein noodles
1	tbs.	Sesame seeds, toasted
2	doz.	Snow peas, julienned

Hints: An unusual combination for a pasta dish.

The fresh Chow Mein noodles can be found in most Asian markets fresh or frozen.

Con't....

INSTRUCTIONS:
Mix the first six ingredients. Then carefully add the chili paste to your liking. Toss in the orange zest and stir with a wire whip to incorporate well. Cook the noodles in boiling water for about 1 1/2 minutes or until they turn limp. Drain. Toss with the dressing and place on the plate with tongs-so excess dressing has a chance to fall off. Garnish the top of each mound of noodles with toasted sesame seeds and julienned snow peas.

Passionate rice

Serves: 4

INGREDIENTS:

1	CUP	White basmati rice
2	TBS.	Shallots, chopped
2	TBS.	Onions, julienned
3	TBS.	Black Chinese rice
1	EACH	Bay leaf
3	OZ.	Pineapple juice
2	OZ.	Olive oil
1	STALK	Scallions, chopped
4	STALKS	Asparagus, sliced-1/4" on a bias
2	OZ.	Pineapple, diced
1	EACH	Passionfruit, pulp
2	TBS.	Almonds, sliced, blanched
2	TBS.	Coconuts, shredded
2	TBS.	Bell peppers, assorted colors
2	OZ.	Bean sprouts
2	OZ.	Snow peas, sliced thinly on a bias
As needed		Salt and pepper, 5:1 ratio

Hints:

This is the dish that goes great with chicken, duck and seafood.

Also, you have to cook the rice separately or the white rice will turn grey.

Toss the veggies in after they are cooked in oil.

INSTRUCTIONS:
Cook the basmati rice with the shallots with 1 1/2 times the amount of water (or chicken consomme) per volume as rice. Cook the black rice with the onions and bay leaf, and 3 1/2 times as much water with the addition of the pineapple juice. Cool slightly. Fork to separate. Then garnish with next half the recipe

NEXT:
    Cook all the veggies in a little oil. Add the rest of the ingredients to the sautee and then add to the rice. Toss well. Check seasons and add more if needed.
    ***** Use 1/2 cup cooked rice per entree.

Plantains

Serves: 6

INGREDIENTS:

3	each	Green plantains
As needed		Salt and white pepper
As needed		Peanut oil
1	cup	Mango-seville vinaigrette, see page 73
1	each	Yolk of an egg

INSTRUCTIONS:

While oil is heating, slice the plantains 1/4 inch thick lengthwise. Deep fry at 375 degrees. until they are golden and crisp. Drain on paper towels. Season. Make the emulsified Mojo style vinaigrette (by blending in a cuisinart) with an addition of the egg yolk. Save until ready to serve. Use the sauce for dipping plantains.

TO USE:

You can also use the plantains as scoops for salads, dips, etc....

HINTS:

Green plantains are harder to peel than ripe ones. Using a spoon, slip the edge of the spoon under the skin and peel back the green outer skin.

Roasted Garlic-Plantain Fritters

Serves: 6

Ingredients:

5	each	Garlic kernels, roasted
1	each	Plantain, green, chopped
As needed		Salted water
As needed		Flour
As needed		Salt and pepper
1/4	cup	Roasted corn kernels
1/4	teas.	Baking powder
2	each	Eggs, separated
As needed		Cream, to moisten
1/2	cup	Orange blossom honey
As needed		Peanut oil
1/4	teas.	Baking powder

Hints:

This dish is great as a fried dumpling to serve along with seafood or poultry.

When caramelizing honey, be quick and careful. Honey will burn your fingers and tongue if you don't let them cool a little first.

Instructions:

Cook the garlic kernels in oil in a heavy bottom pot until well browned. Boil rough chopped plantains in salted water. When tender, remove and drain well. Separate eggs. Whip the whites very stiff. Mash the cooked plantains and cool. Add the yolks and everything else, mix well (except the whites, cream and oil). Lightly fold in the whites. Check the consistency of the batter and add the cream to loosen if needed to make the batter like a thick flap jack batter.

Deep-fry dollops of this batter in 350 degree peanut oil (the same oil the garlic was cooked in). Drain and place on a serving plate.

Note:

Use the nonstick skillet to caramelize the honey. Heat the pan until super hot. Pour in the honey and let boil rapidly. Tilt pan and shake to prevent burning. Quickly drizzle hot over the fritters on the plate.

Potato Planks in Onion and Balsamic

Serves: 4

Notes:
This is one of those recipes that came to me by accident.

Ingredients:

1	recipe	Onion crust, see recipe page 84
3	oz.	Butter, clarified
2	tbs.	Balsamic vinegar
2	oz.	Honey, orange blossom
2	each	Idaho potatoes, quartered and blanched

Instructions:

Peel and quarter the potatoes lengthwise. Blanch in a steamer until a toothpick can be inserted easily. Remove planks and cool enough to handle. Meanwhile make the onion crust. Melt the butter and use only the clarified portion for dipping.

Take the planks and dip them into 3 oz. butter and then the crust. Bake at 375 degrees until fully browned. While this is in the oven, caramelize the honey in a nonstick pan. Then quickly toss in the vinegar. Let this reduce to a thickened syrup consistency. Delicately drizzle over the planks when they come out of the oven.

BogBerry Sweet Potato Terrine

Serves: 10

Ingredients:

40	oz.	Sweet potato, chopped
4	oz.	Fresh cranberries, blanched soft
2	tbs.	Ginger, smashed
1/3	cup	Shallots, sweated in butter
4	oz.	Walnuts, chopped
1 1/2	tbs.	Thyme, chopped
3	tbs.	Cilantro, chopped
1	tbs.	Pink peppercorns, crushed
As needed		Cornmeal, very fine ground
6	oz.	Butter, clarified

Instructions:

Cook the sweet potatoes in water until soft. Drain and while still hot, toss with the rest of the ingredients - except the cornmeal. Cool batch in refrigerator. When chilled scoop portions of mix and place in 2 1/2" wide by 2" tall ring mold. Press down on the mixture while lifting the mold up to release the cake onto a work surface.

Place this cake into the cornmeal to coat both top and bottom of the cake. Place cakes in the freezer just long enough to hardened and make them more manageable.

When ready to use

Heat a little butter in heavy bottom saute pan. Place the cakes in the pan and saute slowly to crisp the cake. Remove and place on sheet pan. Bake for 20 minutes at 375 degrees or until warm in the middle. Use a flat spatula to lift off the pan, The cornmeal crust helps to keep the bottom crisp and stiff enough to remove.

Hints:

I have used American sweet potatoes for this recipe.

I think using Boniato could be a great dish as well for roast duck or, as a base to stack high flavored fish fillets upon.

Sushi Rice

Serves: 10 individual side dish portions

Ingredients:
1	cup	Short grain, sushi rice
1 3/4	cups	Water
2	oz.	Rice vinegar
2	oz.	Mirin
As needed		Salt and white pepper

Instructions:
Wash the rice for a few minutes under running water. Bring the rice and all the rest of the ingredients to a boil. Lower heat, cover pot and simmer rice until all the water is absorbed. Stir rice for the first minute of boiling so the grains separate and don't stick to the bottom of the pot and burn. Cook (slowly) until the water is absorbed. About 15 minutes. Remove from pan. Let cool slightly so it is easier to use.

To Use:
Wet your hands before rolling out sushi or to form into disks for special preparations. I always like to place this rice into a ring mold, flatten and form into a tower of rice. Then top with flying fish roe (Tobiko caviar).
   The Tobiko is layered on top of the tower like a hat. The orange color Tobiko makes for a dramatic visual effect and this preparation and is perfect with a rare seared tuna loin entree.

Hints:

When cooking the rice, use a heavy bottom pot to distribute heat to cook the rice evenly.

This recipe is the base for others that can be made by adding various amounts of garnishes, such as: carrot, celery, pepper bruniose, pickled ginger, chives, apples, citrus, Asian pear, Adzuki beans, etc...

Sun-Natured Rice

Serves: 10

INGREDIENTS:

1/2	CUP	White rice, raw
1/2	CUP	Basmati rice, raw
1/2	CUP	Wild rice, see hints
2	CUPS	Chicken stock, seasoned
2	EACH	Bay leaf
2	TBS.	Sun dried cranberries
1/2	OZ.	Almonds, toasted
2	OZ.	Peppers, assorted, diced
2	OZ.	Onions, diced
1	TBS.	Garlic, chopped finely
2	TBS.	Parsley
1	TEAS	Cilantro, chopped

Hints:

This is one of my favorite side dishes.

Cook the wild rice separately because the wild rice takes more water to cook and will darken the white rice. Toss together later after cooking.

INSTRUCTIONS:

Bring the white rices (including the Basmati) to a boil in a pot atop the stove in the seasoned chicken stock and bay leaf until all the liquid is evaporated. Then cover, and place in a 375 degree oven and cook for 20 minutes more. Remove and flake out the rice onto a sheet pan and cool.

As this is cooking...cook the wild rice in 2 1/2 times the volume of water as the volume of raw wild rice until the grass seeds (wild rice) are puffed slightly and tender to the touch. Cool slightly.

To Use:

When all the rice is done, toss in a large bowl with the rest of the ingredients. Toss and reheat in a wok to warm. The heat from the wok helps bring out the toasted pecan scent of Basmati rice.

Wasabi smashed Bliss potatoes

Serves: 10

Ingredients:

30	each	Baby red potatoes, 1/4'ed
1	tbs.	Wasabi powder, plus two tbs.
As needed		Water to cover potatoes
As needed		Salt and white pepper
1/2	teas.	Pink peppercorns, crushed fine
2	tbs.	Chives, chopped
1	oz.	Basic vinaigrette
1	each	Spanish onion, julienned

Hints:
Pre-cook the potatoes in salted water until a fork can easily be slid in and out of the potatoes. Pink peppercorns makes this a unique dish in and of itself.

Instructions:
Boil the quartered potatoes and onions together in enough water to cover. Add the first tablespoon of wasabi powder to the water before boiling. Cook then drain well. Season the potatoes with salt and white pepper after they come out of the water. Cool slight-just enough so you can easily work with them. Add the second two tablespoon of wasabi powder and the rest of the ingredients.

Toss the potatoes gently so all seasonings are well distributed. While the potatoes are still a little warm, spoon them into a 2" wide by 2" tall stainless steel ring mold with the tube resting on a flat surface. Smash them down into the tube with your fingers or the back side of a wooden spoon. Remove the potatoes from the tube by lifting up on the tube and applying pressure to the potato mixture inside the tube. When the tube is clear from the potato stack, place the resulting potato tower on a greased baking sheet and place it into the refrigerator to firm up for about one hour.

To Use:
Place potato stacks in a 400 degree oven. Bake about 15 minutes or until the inside when tested is warm.

Sweet Potato Spears

Serves: 4

Ingredients:
2	EACH	Sweet potatoes, spear-cut
1	TBS.	Sesame oil
1	TBS.	Shallots
1/2	TEAS.	Thyme, chopped finely
2	OZ.	Maple syrup
1/2	TEAS.	Black and white sesame seeds

Instructions:
After cutting the potato spears, bake at 350 degrees covered, until just softened. Test by inserting a fork. If it smoothly goes in with some resistance they are ready. Uncover. Heat oil and add the shallots. Let cook until soft. Add the thyme and syrup. Let boil a minute. Cool slightly and pour over the potatoes. Bake again uncovered until soft cooked and slightly caramelized. Garnish with seeds.

Hints: You will find that if you slightly under-cook the potatoes, they will be easier to move when ready to place them on a service plate.

Quinoa Salad

Serves: 6

Ingredients:
2	CUPS	Water
2	TBS.	Shallots, diced finely
As needed		Salt and pepper, 5:1 ratio
1	CUP	Quinoa
1/3	CUP	Garlic chive blossoms
1/4	CUP	Tarragon buds
2	EACH	Scallions, sliced on a bias
1/2	EACH	Red bell pepper, small diced
1/4	CUP	Parsley, chopped
1/2	CUP	Ginger-citrus dressing, see recipe page 72

Instructions:
Boil water with the shallots and salt and pepper. Add the Quinoa and cook no longer than 15 minutes. Remove and drain excess water. Add the chopped veggies and the buds. Add a little dressing and toss lightly. Place on the serving plate.

Hints: Quionoa is an Ancient grain. Its roots go back to the Incan empire. A thousand years before Columbus, Quinoa was a favorite side dish for dinner in South America.

Berry Rice - *Wheatberries*
Serves: 6

Ingredients:
2	tbs.	Butter
1	tbs.	Olive oil
1	each	Garlic
1	cup	Basmati rice
3	cups	Water
1/3	cup	Wheatberries, cooked, see below
1/4	cup	Pinenuts
2	teas.	Tamari
1/4	cup	Mixed herbs-equal amounts

Notes:
Your mixed herbs should contain tarragon, basil, thyme, chervil.

In most cases, this dish will work with any seafood dish in this book.

Instructions:
Wash the rice. Sweat the first three ingredients for five minutes. Add the rice, stir and then add 1 1/2 times amount of water to rice. Bring to a boil, and then simmer 15 minutes. Drain. Toss and add the herbs (equal amounts of each herb should be used). Add the nuts, wheatberries and tamari. Toss well. Serve warm.

*** Wheatberries: cook for 25 minutes in two times the volume of water to berrys.

Grilled Veggies
Serves: 8

Ingredients:
1/4	cup	Apple juice
2	tbs.	Balsamic vinegar
1	tbs.	Pommery (grainy) mustard
As needed		Salt and pepper, 5:1 ratio
2	med. size	Eggplant, sliced 3/4 inch thick
2	large	Sweet onion-Maui, sliced
4	each	Red bell pepper, chunks
1	each	Zucchini, sliced 1/2 inch thick
1	each	Yellow squash, like zucchini
8	each	Rosemary skewers, see note

Hints:
To make the rosemary skewers, take thick branches of rosemary and trim off all the leaves (except for the very top plume). Then use to thread the veggies.

Instructions:
Mix the first four ingredients. Dip the veggies into this mix and then grill to your liking. Brush the veggies as they cook with the leftover marinade. Thread the cooked veggies onto the skewers and place on the serving plate.

Yucca Dumplings

Serves: 6

Cook in a lemongrass broth for that light Asian spark needed for snapper or any seafood stew.

Ingredients:

2	stalks	Lemongrass, rough chopped
1	cup	Yucca, *cooked*
1	oz.	Garlic, chopped fine
1/2	teas.	Thyme, choped fine
2	tbs.	Shallots, diced finely
As needed		Salt and pepper, 5:1 ratio
2	each	Scallions, sliced on a bias
2	tbs.	Red bell pepper, small diced
2	tbs.	Flour
1/2	teas.	Baking powder
1/4	cup	Cilantro, chopped
2	bs.	Oil

Hints:

Sprinkle the chopped cilantro over the Yucca.

Also, use this in all sorts of braised dishes that call for stewing the protein in a flavorful stock to finish its cooking.

Instructions:

Boil 1 gallon of water with the lemongrass for 10 minutes to infuse the cooking medium. If you can't find lemongrass, use the rind from a lemon or lime instead. Mix the rest of the ingredients together. Drop tablespoon size dollops of this mixture into the boiling stock. Cook until they float. Taste one to make sure of the seasoning. Drain, coat with a little oil and garnish with the cilantro.

INDEX

A
ACCOLADES OF SALADS....68
ACHIOTE VINAIGRETTE....70
AMERICAN REGIONAL CUISINE....4
ANNATTO.....16, 143
ANNONA....24
APPALACH....118
APPALACHICOLA.....118
ARKIN, STARFRUIT....27
ASPARAGUS, PURPLE....18
ATEMOYA.....16, 25
AWAK, NATIVES...16
AZUKI BEANS....164

B
BARBADOS CHERRY...16
BATIDO....16
BAY SCALLOPS...119
BBQ CURE...81
BBQ MEAT RUB....81
BEAN COOKERY....163
BREADFRUIT....16
BLACK BEANS, HEART OF PALM SALAD....66
BLACK SAPOTE....16
BLUE-CRAB, INDIAN RIVER....118
BOGGY BAY....128
BONAITO....16, 26
BREADFRUIT....16, 38

BOUCHEES, SMALL BITES: 37-53
BRINE....16
BRUNOISE, KNIFE CUT....64

C
CALABAZA, SQUASH....16, 32
CALAMARI....43, 46
CALAMONDINE....16, 99
CAMPBELL, DR....12
CANISTEL....16
CARAMBOLA....27
CHERIMOYA....16, 25
CHILI-COCOA DUST....82
CHIMI-CHURRI....82
CITRUS-PEAR VINAIGRETTE....73
COLADA....17
CONCH, BAHAMIAN....119
COOKING ESSENTIALS.....15
COOKING INGREDIENTS, NEW.....16-18
COULIS-GRETTE....16
CRABCAKES, ST. BARTS....39-42
CRITTER FRITTERS....44
CULINARY USES....23-36

D
DASHEEN....17
DAVID FAIRCHILD, DR......13
DECO....78-83
DUPLICATING FOODWAYS....77-78

E
EDIBLE FLOWERS....67-68

F
FAMILIAR BREEDS CONTEMPT...8
FEATHERS AND BONES: 142-156
   ADOBE POULTRY....143
   ANAHEIM CHICKEN....144
   BBQ RIBS, SPICY GUAVA....153
   CHICKEN, CARIBBEAN-LATINO....144
   CHICKEN, FIRE-ROASTED ONIONS....145
   CHICKEN, PEACH COULIS, GRILLED....146
   DUCK, GREEN TEA MARINATED....149
   DUCK, LACQUERED....147
   DUCK, MOULADE, CITRUS-COFFEE....148
   PORK, MANGO....150
   PORKLOIN, DOVYALIS....154
   PORKLOIN, PECAN SMOKED....151
   PO-POO PLATTER, SOFLO....152
   TURKEYLOIN, FIRE-ROASTED....155
   VEAL CHOPS. ROASTED....156

FLORIDA AGRILCULTURE....21-23
FLORIDA BLISS POTATO SALAD....59
FLORIDA FACTS....21
FLORIDA FRUIT PRODUCTION....21
FLORIDA KEYS....119
FLORIDA AGRICULTURE CHALLENGES....22
FLORIDA POLENTA, GRITS.....17
FWANG TUNG, STARFRUIT....27

G
GINGER-CITRUS VINAIGRETTE....72
GOAT'S CHEESE....52
GOLDEN STAR, STARFRUIT....27
GRAIN COOKERY....161-162
GRILLING TECHNIQUES....17
GRITS AND GRUNTS....17
GUAVAS....17, 28, 103, 153
GUARAPO....17

H
HADEN, MANGO....31
HEART OF PALM....34
HERB OIL....135
HERBENA-CHIMICHURRI....83
HURRICANE ANDREW....55

I
ILLAMA....25
INDIAN RIVER....118
INFUSIONS....17
INSIGHTS AND BACKGROUND...11

J
JABOTICOBA....17
JACKSONVILLE, SHRIMP....119
JICAMA-MELON SALAD....61
JOURNEY BEGINS, THE....6

K
KAMPONG, THE....13
KEITT, MANGO...31
KENT, MANGO.....31
KIMCHEE, GREEN PAPAYA....60-61
KUMQUATS....17

INDEX

L
LEMONGRASS....17
LICHEE....17, 29, 52
LOBSTER AND MUSHROOM FILO....44, 45, 46
LOBSTER, SPINY....119
LONGAN....17
LOQUAT....17

M
MACADAMIA NUTS....18
MALANGA....18, 30
MAMEY....18, 144
MANGO....31, 48, 105, 125, 128
MANGO MAYO....72
MANGO-SEVILLE COULIS...73
MANGO-YOGURT DRESSING, CURRIED....75
MANGOS, SPICY GLAZED....48
MANGOS, TOASTY CRISPY....48
MARK TWAIN....24
MAYPOP, FRUIT....33
MIAMI, THE TELFON CITY....12
MOJO....18
MORNING MARKET, THE....56=57

N
NEW AMERICAN RIVIERA....78-80
NEW WORLD, FRUIT....24
NEW WORLD SQUASH....32

O
OLD SOUR....18
OMEGA-THREE....114
ONION CRUST....84
OPAL-BASIL VINAIGRETTE....73
ORANGE, SEVILLE....18

P
PAPAYA SALSA....50
PASSION OF A CHEF.....5
PASSIONFRUIT....33, 74, 108
PASSIONFRUIT-CHIPOTLE VINAIGRETTE....74
PORTABELLA CRAB SANDWICH....51
PROTHICK, FOOD STARCH....74

Q
QUAIL SALAD, JACKFRUIT....63

R
RADDICCHIO, GRILLED WITH CRAB....64
REDLANDS, THE....55-56, 125
REDUCTIONS....18
REPERTOIRE. LE....76-89
ROCK SHRIMP....119
ROLLINIA....25

S
SABLE PALM....34
SADODILLA....18
SALADS: 54-75
   FLORIDA BLISS POTATO SALAD....59
   SPA VEGGIE ANTIPASTO....58
   WASABI CUCUMBERS....60
SALAD ACCOLADES....68-69
SALAD ARRANGEMENTS....67
SALAD BASICS.....67
SALAD ESSENTIALS...66
SALAD MAKINGS....67
SALAD MATH....69
SALAD TEMPTATIONS....67-68
SALMON MARINADE....84
SALSA, PAPAYA....50
SAUCES: 90-112
   APRICOT-GINGER GLAZE....95
   ANAHEIM-VANILLA SYRUP....95
   APPLE CIDER SAUCE-SOFLO STYLE....98
   CALAMONDINE SAUCE....99
   CILANTRO AIOLI....99-100
   CHERIMOYA BEURRE BLANC....100
   RED CURRY, GRAPEFRUIT AND GUAVA....101
   EXOTIC FRUIT SAUCE....102
   GUAVA BBQ BASTING SAUCE....103
   GUAVA GLAZE, SPICY....103-4
   JABOTICABA GLAZE....104
   LEMONGRASS AND SOURSOP....105
   MANGO BEURRE BLANC....105
   MUSTARD SEED SAUCE, SPROUTED....106
   ORANGE-MAPLE-ALLSPICE SAUCE....106-7
   ORANGE SAUCE, SMOKED....107
   FIVE-SPICE PAPAYA BBQ SAUCE....107-8
   PASSIONFRUIT SAUCE, SIMPLE....108
   PEACH-ORANGE COULIS....108-9
   PO-POO SAUCE...109
   SOURSOP SAUCE....110
   STARFRUIT ESSENCE....110
   THAI SPRITZ, ESSENCE....111
   YELLOW TOMATO SAUCE, SMOKED....112
   VANILLA, REAL STUFF....112
STRIPED BASS, HERBENA....136
STRIPED BASS, MACADAMIA NUT CRUSTED....136

SEAFOOD: 113-141
   BANANA BASS....123
   BLACK GROUPER, SOFRITO CRUSTED....126
   COBIA, WITH SALSA, SMOKED....123-4
   GROUPER, SOUTHWESTERN CRUSTED....126
   MANGO SEABASS, BLACKENED....128
   MAKO SHARK, BLACK PEPPER CRUSTED....137
   REDLANDS BLACK GROUPER....125
   SCALLOPS CALAMONDINE....127
   SCALLOPS, SEARED....129
   SCALLOPS, STARFRUIT-THAI CRUST....127

   SEABASS, CHIMICHURRI BEURRE BLANC....130
   SNAPPER, THAI-BASIL CRUSTED...133

INDEX

Shrimp, corn crusted....134
Shrimp, rack of....135
Souffle fish fingers....132
Swordfish, Asian-pear....139
Swordfish, tamarind-jerk....138
Tuna, sesame seared....140
Wahoo....140
Yellowtail, simple....141
Yellowtail, plantain crusted....141
Seafood, buying.....115
Seafood characteristics, chart....122
Seafood, health benefits....124
Seafood, judging....116
Seafood, creole seasonings...83
Seafood spice rub...85
Seafood usage....115-6
Seville orange....18, 73
Shellac....18
Shellfish, for seafood lovers....126-128
Shiitaki Mushroom....19
Shrimp, curry grilled....50
Sofrito...88
Soursop....18, 25
South Florida Aquaculture....117
South Western crust....85
Spa Cuisine....18, 19
Spa Veggie Antipasto....58
Starchy Things, Veggies: 157-182
    Azuki beans....164
    Black-eyed peas....165
    Black bean, compote...165
    Cou-Cou....170
    Cous-cous, spiced....169
    Chick peas salad....167
    Citrus noodles....171
    Coconut rice...167
    Fusion pasta....171
    Maytag blue potatoes....166
    Passionate rice...172
    Plantains....173
    Plantains, roasted garlic....174
    Potato planks, onion and balsamic....175
    Quinoa salad....180
    Sweet potato terrine, bogberry....176
    Sun-natured rice....178
    Sushi rice....177
    Sweet potato spears....180
    Veggies, grilled....181
    Wasabi bliss potatoes....179
    Wheatberry rice....181
    White bean compote....169
    Yucca dumplings....182

St. Barts, crabcake.....39-42

Starches....160-162
Star King, starfruit....27
Stone Crab and Calabaza fritters...49
Stoners, harvesting....121
Sugar Apple....25

Swamp Cabbage....34
Sweet Sop....25

T

Tamarind pod, fruit.....35
Tampa, clams...120
Taste, paradigns in flavor....90-3
Taste, scientific look....91
Taste-Variance....91-3
Teflon City, the.....12
Thayer, starfruit....27
Thai-Knight, starfruit....27
Titusville....119
Tommy Akins....31
Tropical Cookery provisions....20
Tropical Cuisinier, the....3
Tuna....140

U

Underneath a cloudless sky...4
Uglifruit....18, 36,
Uglifruit coulis-grette....74-5

V

Van Dyke, mango....32
Vegan fried truffles....53

W

Wahoo....122, 140
Wasabi cucumbers....60
Wild poultry rub....88

XYZ

Xanthan Gum, food thickener....70
Yin and Yang marinade....89
Yougans, starfruit....27
Yucatan spice rub....89
Zip, the.....65

NOTES:

Don't forget about our other books see our website at:
www.FoodBrats.com

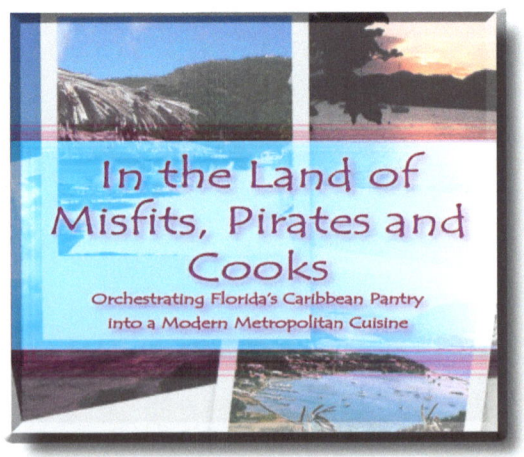

180 pages, 125 recipes
and 50 FULL color pictures

www.ingramcontent.com/pod-product-compliance
Lightning Source LLC
Chambersburg PA
CBHW041514220426
43668CB00002B/18